S0-AKZ-061

The
First Week™
with
My New
Digital
Camera

The
First Week™
with
My New
Digital
Camera

A Very Basic Guide to Understanding,
Editing, and Saving Digital
Photographs

Pamela R. Lessing

Capital Books, Inc.
Sterling, Virginia

Copyright © 2003 by Pamela R. Lessing

All rights reserved. No part of this book may be reproduced or utilized in any form or by any means, electronic or mechanical, including photocopying, recording, or by any information storage and retrieval system, without permission in writing from the publisher. Inquiries should be addressed to:

Capital Books, Inc.
P.O. Box 605
Herndon, Virginia 20172-0605

Notice of Liability
The information in this book is distributed on an "As is" basis, without warranty. While every precaution has been taken in preparation of the book, neither the author nor Capital Books shall have liability to any person or entity with respect to any losses or damage caused or alleged to be caused directly or indirectly by the instructions contained in this book or by the software and hardware described in it.

Trademarks and Copyrights
The following trademarks are used with permission of Microsoft, Jasc Software™, ACD™ System, Ltd., and Adobe Systems, and are used only in an editorial fashion and to the benefit of the trademark owner. No intention of infringement of the trademark is meant. ACDSee™ 5.0, ACD™ Systems, Ltd., Acrobat® Reader™ Adobe® Photoshop® Elements 2.0, Adobe® Systems, CompactFlash® card, FotoCanvas™, HotSync®, Jasc Software™, Microsoft® Picture It!®, Microsoft® PowerPoint®, Microsoft® QuickTime™, Palm OS® PDAs, Smart Media™ card, Sony Memory Stick®, The First Week™, Windows®, Zip® disk.

Library of Congress Cataloging-in-Publication Data
Lessing, Pamela R.
    The first week with my new digital camera: a very basic guide to understanding, editing, and saving digital photographs / Pamela R. Lessing.
      p. cm.
    ISBN 1-931868-17-4
    1. Digital cameras. 2. Photography—Digital techniques. 1. Title.
TR256.L47 2003
778.3–dc21

                                      2003001573

Book design by Ellen Banker
Cartoons by David Shenton

Printed in the United States of America on acid-free paper that meets the American National Standards Institute Z39-48 Standard.

First Edition

10 9 8 7 6 5 4 3 2

To All My Children

Beth, Paul, David, Scott, Johan, Anne, and Pad.
Your love, caring, enthusiasm, and wonderful
achievements are a joy to all of us.

To My Sister, Joan

Your kind words and deeds are never forgotten.

To All My True Friends

From Vail and Boulder to Bhutan, your friendships,
involvement, and encouragement have helped us
immeasurably, and we love you all.

Also by Pamela R. Lessing

First Week™ Series

Popular how-to manuals by the master
of non-patronizing instructions
for the Digital Age

The First Week™ with My New PC
The First Week™ with My New Mac
The First Week™ with My New Digital Organizer

Contents

Acknowledgments

At this time, my first thoughts go to my publisher, Kathleen Hughes. She is always available, answers her own telephone, and is calm and relaxed, in spite of all that must be happening around her. She is ready to spend a few minutes chatting, handles any of my difficulties herself, and finds humor in the most bizarre situations. She does all this with an elegance that must inspire her staff. The people at Capital Books follow this leadership with enthusiasm, and I appreciate all their hard work, too.

As each manuscript nears completion, my first telephone call is to London and my wonderful illustrator, David Shenton. The words are all written down, and this is the time to discuss the peculiarities and funny thoughts that we have about this latest piece of technology. He translates all this, with wit and flair, into the most amusing cartoons to enhance each point. I am very fortunate to work with the very best and to know him as a friend.

Additional thanks go to Richard Harman. Circumstances made it difficult for me to understand and appreciate all the nuances of each of the digital camera programs, and it was Rich who helped me piece it all together. He was able to answer my questions, which, I hope, means that I will have covered all of yours. It is not an easy task to "Capture" all the screen shots or figures that you see in this book. It takes special skills. It was Jeff Shuenke who worked with me to follow my text and clarify many of these points. I thank him for his invaluable help.

Many people suggested topics for the fourth book in this series. None was as persuasive as General John T. Chain when he insisted that my next book had to teach him what to do with all the digital photographs he had sitting on his computer. The

Chains were the first to receive a copy of the manuscript, check out all the parameters, and see if "it would fly." I know that I could not have had two better test pilots than Jack Chain and his wife, Judie Chain, a model of strength blended with graciousness and charm, and I thank them for their time and hard work.

I also wish to thank Betsy Friess, and Bob and Sylvia Gordon, other friends who were always asking questions and reminding me of areas that needed to be covered. Their enthusiasm for testing my directions and providing the right feedback helped enormously.

My family did a wonderful job of adjusting to a very different schedule this time around. I hope we all feel that we were available to each other whenever needed, and that we handled the ups and downs of life well. I am very proud of all of you. And to my 88-year-old mother, Helen D.K. Lessing: *Yes*, you have to read the book. *No*, you do not have to buy either a PDA or a digital camera—you can use mine!

Introduction

This is the fourth in a series of books called *The First Week*™, and that is exactly what I am talking about. The very *first* week with your new computer, personal digital assistant, or in this case, the first week with your new digital camera. For some reason, a very small percentage of people feel that it is important to have an introduction to give people an understanding and "feel" for the tone and information in the rest of the book. I have found from personal experience (and writing these books) that, in fact, approximately one person out of 3,428 will actually read these words. Therefore, if you are one of the few people who have opened the book to this section, and you want to learn why you should buy this book, I apologize for not taking the Introduction more seriously.

I always give my e-mail address at the end of the introduction so that people can comment or ask questions related to *The First Week* book that they are reading. In this case I shall give it to you right now, at the beginning of the Introduction, so you do not have to wait. It is prlessing@bigfoot.com. Now you have it immediately available if you want to send me your comments and thoughts.

The fact is, you really will learn a great deal by reading this book. The first thing to bear in mind is that while most of us are familiar with cameras and are comfortable with *taking* a photograph, the real issue is what to do once we have captured an image. How many times have you used one of those "travel" paper cameras or shot a roll of film only to wait several weeks (or, to be truthful, several months) before going to have the film developed? (This is the moment when you have forgotten what is on the film, and you are really full of curiosity. Now you take the rolls of film to the "one-hour processing" place and pay extra because you need to see them *immediately*!) My point is that it does not matter if you are experienced or inexperienced with print or slide photography, or whether you have decided to plunge right into the market with the latest technology. The purpose of this book is to tell you what to do *once you have actually taken a digital photograph.*

This is really rather simple in some ways. After all, your camera came with a set of instructions as to how to transfer the images from the camera into your computer. However, there are several ways to do this, as this book will explain. Again, for most of us, the real question is how do you take all of these images, edit them, and make them "usable"? That is exactly what I shall explain.

The first part of the book covers some of the basics of digital photography, including formats, resolution, editing tools, and common terms. This is followed by several chapters that describe how to use a number of the most popular and basic photo editing software programs currently available. Each of these programs will teach you how to do primary image corrections. These corrections will make the photograph you are viewing look just as you wish you had taken it "at the time." That is one of the many great things about digital photography. You can be just like all the movie directors and newspaper and magazine editors (and, some people would add, special government organizations), who take digital images and correct them so that everything looks just as they think it should look. Go ahead. Turn the page to whichever chapter interests you. It is time to get started!

1

Chapter 1
Let's Start at the Beginning: Advantages, Disadvantages, and Just Getting Started

The First Week with My New Digital Camera

As I stated in the Introduction, the purpose of this book is to teach you what to do with the digital photographs you have produced. That means how to actually take the photographs you have created "off of the camera" and get those images into your computer, how to edit the images, and then how to do creative things with your edited pictures. I would like to assume that you already own a digital camera. However, this might not be the case, and so this is the moment to consider your needs when choosing a digital camera. Needless to say, this includes looking at the positive and negative aspects of your new (or future) gift or purchase.

As you do when you contemplate purchasing any new piece of equipment, you have probably given much thought as to what your needs might be, how much money you want to spend on this item, and how it "works" for you. In the case of a digital camera, there are more models on the market than most of us have time to examine personally. To some extent, it is easy to figure out how much money you want to spend (unless you are easily seduced by salespeople). As for your needs, I think that you will find at least a few compelling reasons for buying a digital camera on the list of "positive aspects" below. But first I want to talk about what I mean by "how it 'works' for you."

As with anything in your life, your new digital camera has to "feel good" to *you*. You sit in a car and test drive it, you measure a couch and sit on it, and you listen to a number of stereo systems before picking out the one that sounds the best to you. It is the same with digital cameras. The one you choose has to feel good in your hands—not too big and heavy for you to hold easily, or too small for you to work the controls and see everything clearly.

It is important for you to see the images you are trying to capture. This means that you need to consider the different viewfinders. If you are used to looking through an optical viewer, like the ones on non-digital cameras, you might want to get a camera that has this feature along with the Liquid Crystal Display (LCD) screen that is standard with most good-quality digital cameras. (Personally, I find that another reason for having both is that sometimes it is difficult to see the LCD screen in bright lighting conditions.) And why do you want a camera with an LCD screen? This is one of the best features of a digital camera. With an LCD screen you can immediately see the photo you have taken. This lets you retake the bad ones and make whatever corrections you need in order to get the best images possible.

You want a camera that has the features you think you currently need, but you are spending a lot of money and might want to think about future needs, too. Some people only want a camera for e-mailing photographs of family events, trips, or the new baby. Most people would think that a basic camera would be fine for this. However, just because you are thinking along these lines now, it does not mean that you do not need the ability to control the flash and exposures, the possibility of choosing the amount of optical and/or digital zoom, or the tools to vary the size of each group of images (resolution). These are really rather basic features and will not cost much more. After all, what happens when you get that amazing photograph of all four generations of your family and want to make a nice "photo-quality" print for everyone? Then you will wish you had that 3.3 megapixel camera.

Finally, you will have to consider what kind of "memory card" you want to use. The memory card is where your digital images are stored. It replaces the film you used in your old camera. It seems that many manufacturers have their own proprietary system. However, whatever camera you own, you can buy this same type of card in different memory "sizes," from 8 megabytes (8 MB) to 1 gigabyte (1 G). The larger the number of megabytes on a card, the more images you can put on that card, and the larger resolution format (number of "pixels," or picture elements) you can store per image. As an example, Sony uses something called a Memory Stick®. (This is also known as a "gum stick"—take a look at it and you will see why.) If you own other Sony products such as a computer or a personal digital assistant, you will find it easier to continue with this memory system, and it is will be more cost-effective, too. Physical size is also a consideration when choosing a memory system. While CDs have the advantage of letting you transfer your photographs to the computer easily, they are physically larger than the other memory card formats. This means your camera will have to be larger to accommodate them.

Having said all this, let's consider why you should have a digital camera in the first place. As to which camera to choose—make, model, features—I leave that to you and the salesperson at your camera store. The one suggestion that I do have is that unless you want to do professional photography (in which case you should be at a level where you do not need this book), or you want to make very large prints of your digital images, you probably will be just fine with a camera that can take photographs that are 3.3 megapixels. (See Glossary.)

Now, why enter the world of digital photography?

On the positive side:

- No matter what the price of the camera you chose, you will have a fine piece of equipment that will take very nice photographs with minimum effort.
- Your camera will be totally automatic (referred to as a PHD, or "push here dummy," camera) or it will offer a certain number of manual settings that will allow you to control your "environment." That is important, because it means you will be starting with a good image.
- You will no longer be using film, so whether you use a CompactFlash® Card, a Memory Stick, a SmartMedia

Card™, a CD, or another memory device, you can take more photographs with less hassle.

- You will be able to load all these photographs onto your computer, which means that you can instantly print copies of the good ones, save images on CDs, create albums that you can share over the Internet, send as many as you like to friends and family via e-mail, and create special projects such as greeting cards and newsletters.
- You will be able to vary the number of pixels (picture elements) for your photographs. If you are only e-mailing the photographs, you can choose a setting with fewer pixels (lower resolution); they will be small files that "download" quickly. Photos to be printed can be set to have better (higher) resolution, which means they'll have more pixels per image.
- Depending on which camera you own, you might also be able to take brief videos that are 30 to 60 seconds in length. (To be truthful, this is all that most people really want to see of anyone's videos—remember the 10-minute video of your sister's cat or the endless slide shows of Uncle Harry's trips?)
- And to my mind, the best reason for using a digital camera is that you can see your photographs immediately. This means that if you have taken a bad shot, you can see instantly that you have cut off someone's head or that their eyes were closed, delete that image, and retake it (and retake it and retake it).

On the negative side:

- The primary complaint of most people, and the reason this book was written, is that you are now sitting with 400 photographs in folders on your computer desktop, and you have no idea what to do with them.
- The initial cost of the camera and its "capture medium" (memory card or the like) is more than the cost of simple

35-millimeter film cameras. (However, do not forget that buying, developing, and making extra prints of 35-millimeter film costs money, too.)

- On trips you will need to carry a charging unit (and adapter for travel abroad) instead of a $16.99 battery.
- And finally, it means that you will miss the drive back and forth and your discussions with the cashier at the one-hour photo processing place. (Not to mention the time spent going back to have extra prints made of the three really good photographs in the roll of 24.)

So with all this in mind, let's assume that you have the new camera and have just opened the box. Now what? You have more equipment than you probably expected, and in fact I have some suggestions for additional things you will need. (Yes, in case the person at the photo shop did not already mention or sell these things to you, I will be the one to tell you that you will have to spend a bit more money to have an efficient, easy, and happy experience with your camera.)

The first thing you will probably do is to throw all the paperwork, cables, CDs, and batteries out of the way to look at your wonderful new camera. **Do not misplace any of these things**. You will need most of them immediately. First of all, and I hate to say this as it is the opposite of my own instincts, it really helps to read the manual *first* so that you are putting everything together properly. It may seem obvious where everything goes—the batteries, the memory card, and of course the nice strap that you wear around your neck. The salesperson may even have given you some instruction in all this. But it helps to know how long you need to charge the battery or batteries if the camera uses a lithium ion battery or rechargeable batteries (anywhere from four to twelve hours), which way the memory card goes into its slot, and where to plug things in.

Now, if you have a camera that takes AA non-rechargeable batteries that just pop into the camera so you are ready to go, do not feel too smug at this point. While you can start using your camera immediately, in the long term you will need so many of these batteries that they will probably take up all the room in your camera bag. (My suggestion is that you go ahead, look through your instruction manual, take several photographs, and have fun for a few hours. Then go out and buy rechargeable batteries.)

So what do you do while you are waiting for the batteries to charge?

1. With the camera in front of you, find all the controls that are shown in the first few pages of the user manual. All cameras are different, so I cannot tell you where or how your model will work, but digital cameras tend to have two basic types of controls. There are a number of buttons on the outside of the camera case for the most essential needs, and there is an "on screen" menu for some of the basics (setup, resolution, etc.) and also the fine-tuning.

2. If you have an AC power adapter, plug it into the camera and the electrical outlet and then put in your memory card so you can try taking some photographs. (Again check the owner's manual, but the memory cards usually have little arrows that show the correct way to put them into the slot in the camera. The card usually will not go in if you try to put it in upside down or backwards. **Remember, never force anything**.)

3. Find the CDs that you threw to the side and load them onto your computer. (Place the disks into the disc drive one at a time, and follow the instructions on your screen for adding these programs.) This way your viewer software is already installed in your program file on your computer when you are actually ready to transfer your images from the camera to the computer.

4. Fill in the warranty cards and send in all that stuff so you do not forget to do it or lose anything.

5. If your camera uses regular batteries, they will soon be dead. Go get the rechargeable ones!

If you recall, near the beginning of this chapter I mentioned that your expenses did not end with the purchase of your camera. This statement might be hard to believe and a bit discouraging, but it comes from personal experience. In order to have fun with your camera and enjoy the complete digital photography experience—from taking the photographs to playing with your edited images—in my opinion, you will need to buy the following:

• An extra battery so that you have plenty of power.
• At least one extra memory card. I would suggest two, as the 8 MB or 16 MB one that came with your camera will not get you very far. I also strongly suggest that you buy one with the highest number of megabytes that you can afford. (Actually, the prices of memory cards have come down quite a bit, so considering the cost of your original investment, this should not be too big a deal.)

- A memory card reader (USB connection preferably) for your kind of memory device. Some memory cards can be placed in special floppy discs that work in a similar fashion to the memory card reader, but if you are planning on using the cables that came with your camera, it will take an amazingly long time to download the images from your camera to your computer.
- A new printer (possibly) and maybe even a new computer. Consider what computer and printer you are using. You will need a computer that has at least 128 MB of RAM and a Pentium II processor (or its equivalent). As with many things, power, speed and space are the keys to success. As for the printer, there are many inexpensive printers that will make excellent color copies. One of the important points here is that you need to use good photo-quality paper. Having said this, please remember that what you are looking at on your computer is an image with "unlimited" colors. Your printer (if it is the basic type) is trying to combine the three ink colors in your cartridge into a similar image. Be prepared to "cut it some slack."
- Image-editing software. Basic image-editing software probably came with your computer and possibly with your camera. These programs are truly basic. What you will need to do is find a program that works well for you. Luckily, this is exactly what this book is all about. I have chosen several popular and easy programs for image editing. After reading the chapters for each one, you can decide what seems right for you.
- And finally, buy yourself a nice bag to hold all your new equipment. I personally do not like to have anything that looks too much like a camera bag. I do not want to be "a target," especially when traveling abroad. However, it really does make a difference to have all your gear in something that is comfortable to carry. It also means that you can keep things organized and will not be running

around the house to find a battery charger or that spare lens. (And yes, you might want to get some additional lenses, but I have spent enough of your money for the first week and will not get into these items, too.)

Finally, let me say what has been said to every person who has ever bought a new camera, or rather, what should have been said. Go out and take lots of photographs. Get to know your equipment well before you go on that special trip, drive to the family reunion, or try to capture your child's first anything. It is amazing how many people think that because they have used many cameras before, they will be able to handle this one in a similar way. I tell you this because I was one of those people. I would rather not tell you the number of mistakes I made in the beginning—and still make when I am not paying attention to changing lighting conditions, etc. Let's just say that I am grateful, just as you will be, that digital images can be edited into beautiful photographs. Having said all this, let's move on to the next chapters, where I cover a few more of the basics, including formats, editing tools, and terms.

2

Chapter 2
Some of the Basic Concepts of Digital Imaging: Resolution, Pixels, and Formats

Before I go into all the details of editing digital images, I think it would be helpful for you to know what actually happens when you press the "shutter" button on your digital camera to take a photograph. In addition, I think it would be useful for you to understand why everyone makes such a fuss about image formats like JPEG, TIFF, GIFF, BMP, etc., and what each of these formats actually do in the camera and on your computer. I also think one of the most important questions to clear up is, "What does the word 'pixel' mean, and why it is important to me?" Now if you know all this, or are frantic to get some photographs edited and sent to your family, please feel free to skip ahead to the chapters that interest you. You can always come back to this one later. For the rest, let's try to get a better understanding of the basics of digital photography.

How is the Digital Photograph Taken?

As you may have noticed, I put quotation marks around the word "shutter" in the opening paragraph of this chapter. The reason for this is that a digital camera actually has no shutter. Cameras that use film have a shutter that opens and closes to expose a piece of film (a chemically coated piece of plastic) to light for a brief moment. When, the film is exposed, the various light-sensitive colors in each layer of the film are activated, so that the film captures an image of whatever is there. When you press the button on a regular camera, you actually hear the "click" of the metal shutter opening and closing. Now, I really do not want to get into a discussion of light, film speed (ISO), aperture settings, etc. I have never understood most of that, and therefore I was happy to buy two basic types of film and keep my camera settings to "automatic." (Yes, I confess, I enjoyed the basic "PHD" 35-millimeter cameras.)

With digital cameras, unlike conventional film cameras, it is not the opening and closing of a metal shutter that allows light to enter and imprint an image on a piece of film. Today most digital cameras use what is called a CCD chip. These initials stand for Charged Coupled Device. A CCD chip is a sensor and a computer chip that is a permanent part of your camera. When you press the shutter button on a digital camera, this chip is electronically "turned on," so that the CCD's pixels (picture elements) can register the different levels of light entering the camera. (Each pixel is a tiny, light-sensitive square on the CCD, and all the dots form the image you are photographing.) It is still easier to refer to this as a shutter, as something does open, but the mechanism is different.

The camera is a minicomputer. The information from the CCD chip becomes electrical charges that go through the camera's microprocessor. The microprocessor then changes the charges into digital bits. These digital bits get stored on the memory card. (By the way, this is not the time to get too confused by other aspects of photography. Yes, you still have choices such as aperture settings that can be set on automatic or manual. The aperture is simply the opening that adjusts to allow a certain amount of light to enter the camera. However, I do not think that it is important to go into the details of this right now, as it would take the rest of this chapter to give you all the necessary information.)

So having read all this, you may be wondering why you hear a familiar "click" when you press the shutter button, especially as there is nothing opening and closing in the traditional sense. The word "familiar" is the key word here. We are all used to hearing that special sound, which tells us that a photograph has been taken. Many digital cameras have this sound as a feature that can be turned on or off. If your camera does not make this noise, in the beginning you may find yourself always checking to see if an image has actually been recorded. Therefore I suggest you activate this feature to have one less complication in your life.

Along these lines, there is something else you need to understand in order to use your camera correctly. It actually takes a bit more than a moment for the CCD to record the information. Therefore the idea of pressing the button and immediately turning to take your next photograph can be a problem (unless you change several settings). You may find your images blurred or not properly lighted. Without getting too Zen about all this, give yourself that moment to compose your photograph and then take the time to actually capture the image. (Now I am not stupid. I understand that babies and kittens will not sit still for you to casually "get things together." The answer to this is to keep taking lots of photographs. This is not film, and anything that looks awful can be deleted. Also, if you really want speed, change the settings on your camera so it can meet your needs.)

Image Formats

In digital photography, when an image is recorded onto a memory card, it is not that a real photograph is actually imprinted on this card. Rather, electronic data is placed in a location. These pieces of data are called pixels (picture elements), and they are literally the last things that I want to discuss because they are a difficult concept for many of us to understand. But don't worry, I shall try to explain the concept of pixels at the end of this chapter, and I will also explain why they are probably the most important aspects of taking a really good digital photograph.

What is important to understand in the meantime is that the whole system would not work if there were not standard formats used to record all the data. This data is put on a variety of different memory cards that fit different cameras from many manufacturers. It will then go into computers, which each have their own operating systems. Sounds complicated, right? That is why there are standard formats to record data. It means that no matter which camera, memory card, and computer you use, all the software for reading and using the images will be compatible. While there are many different formats, there are really just a few that are important for your level of digital photography.

The most common file format, and the one all cameras will have as their initial, primary setting, is the JPEG format. JPEG (pronounced "jay peg") is an acronym for Joint Photographic Experts Group. (As a computer file extension it is written .jpg.) In the JPEG file format, the data of each image is compressed. This has the advantage of saving space on the memory card, so more images can be stored. What is the disadvantage? The disadvantage is that some bits of information are lost in the process of compression. (This is the reason that the JPEG format is called "lossy.") Is this really a problem? No, it is not in most cases. A JPEG image records more than 16 million colors and can be seen nicely on the Internet (which has a standard of 256 colors). Also, if you are printing smaller photographs, the loss is almost unnoticeable. The human eye can only see a certain amount of information in each photograph. (In fact, our brain spends a lot of time filling in information for all our senses for us.) For example, you can look at a magazine photograph and think that it is a great picture. If you were to enlarge that picture over and over again, you would now see all the little gaps and jagged edges. But you are not enlarging the picture, the normal size is just fine, and that is the point of the JPEG format. It works for the majority of your photographic needs. In addition, the amount of compression and therefore the amount of loss varies, so this is something you can play with by taking some time to shoot the same image in several formats and looking at the differences. Later you can decide whether you want to consider other formats for special photographs.

If you are interested in making images that can be enlarged to a much greater size (such as 13″ × 19″), then you should consider setting your camera to record in the TIFF format. TIFF stands for Tagged Image File. (It is pronounced the way it looks, and its computer file extension is .tif.) The TIFF format is primarily used when you want to capture and save every part of the image—every bit of the information. In other words, every pixel is saved in the electronic image just as it is viewed in the original image, and there is usually no compression of the image (a "lossless" image). As nothing is lost, the photograph can be reproduced with excellent resolution in larger sizes. The disadvantage is that if you save every bit of information, it means that each image takes up a great deal of space on your memory card. Depending on the resolution size chosen, even a 64 MB or 128 MB memory card might only hold four to eight photos in the TIFF format, while it would manage a couple of hundred in JPEG.

Even though you may take all of your photographs in JPEG format, and you will initially transfer these images to your computer in this format, some people feel that the best thing to do when you are editing your photographs is to convert the files from JPEG to TIFF format. The reason for this is exactly what I described above. JPEG is a compressed format that is "lossy," and TIFF is not. This aspect does not change once the photograph is taken. This means that each time you make a change of some kind in the editing process and hit the *final* "Save" or "Done" button, a little more of the image will be lost because JPEG compresses the image. If you plan to do all of your editing at one time, this does not really make a difference. Each change you make is stored in a temporary file, just as it is when you save a portion of a document. Your changes are saved in levels. It is when you are ready to close the window and are asked whether you want to save the image that all these edits are really made final. If you do not plan to make any other changes, staying in the JPEG format is fine. If it is in the TIFF format, the image can be altered during several editing "sessions" without losing any of the basic information.

Other formats to be aware of include BMP (bit-map) format and GIFF (Graphics Interchange Format). The first is used on

PCs with the Windows® operating system. BMP is not used on the Internet, and one of the reasons for this is that the files are very large. BMP does not compress images at all. The advantage is that it maps the image directly onto the computer screen, pixel per pixel, with nothing to process. (The computer does not have to "imagine" and fill in what it thinks should be included.) One of the main uses of this format today is for editing images and for the background, or "wallpaper," on your computer desktop. The other format, GIFF (pronounced "jiff"), is often used on the Internet, as it can be manipulated to show only portions of an image without covering up the entire window of your web page. [This means that you can add the colors and information you want in other areas of the web page.] It also is easier to download GIFF files. This is a very popular feature, as many people have slow Internet connections. There are many other digital file formats. Most of these are used by professional Web designers and artists, and are not something you will need at the beginning of your digital experience. Initially you will only need to understand JPEG and TIFF, so let's move on to the question of pixels.

Pixels

The word pixel stands for "picture element." In some ways it is a very easy concept to understand. A pixel is a small square. When one places lots (thousands to millions) of these colored squares together, each square shows a color at its own brightness level and in this way it creates an image. That part is simple to understand. What is difficult to understand is that the number of pixels in a photograph can vary. This is where the term and concept of "resolution" becomes important. The resolution of a digital photograph is directly related to the number of pixels in the image. As pixels are compressed or expanded, the quality of the image can change. If you shoot an image with relatively few pixels (to use for e-mailing or a normal 3″ × 5″ print), you would make a 640 × 480 pixel image. This means there are actually 307,200 pixels in this image, enough for a relatively clear snapshot. But if you try to enlarge the image to make an 8″ × 10″ print, the same 307,200 pixels are spread over a much larger area, and the result will be a very bad photograph filled with "jaggies" and "artifacts." (More on these terms later.) This is because the pixels have to be expanded to fill the additional space.

What is actually happening? One way to think about pixels is to imagine a pegboard in which each hole is filled with a colored marble. Each marble represents a pixel. Once you have taken a photograph, the number of pixels is set for that image. As you look at this image on your computer screen, you start with each picture pixel mapped to one screen pixel. If you want to make the image larger and zoom in, you are now putting several "virtual" marbles around the one hole to try to create one single square that is similar to the original square. Another way of thinking about this is that where there was one photo pixel, there are now four screen pixels. The opposite of this is to zoom out if you want to make the image smaller. However, this is a problem because you are now trying to push a lot of marbles into the original single hole. What happens in either situation is that there is loss of detail.

Resolution

That brings us to the concept of resolution, which is directly connected to pixels. Resolution is the number of pixels that actually make the image you see. Understanding resolution is extremely important, because this is the feature of your digital photography that you can control completely. When you decide to get a digital camera, the first question for you to consider should be, How will I use this camera? If the primary purpose is to send photos on the Internet or to make 3″ × 5″ prints, then an inexpensive camera with 1 megapixel capability is fine. A camera like this can only capture images that are "low resolution." What this means is that each image will capture a maximum of 1 million pixels. Because of the limited number of pixels, the reproduction size of each image will be limited.

Earlier I talked about what happens if you want to enlarge the image that you have already taken and there are not enough pixels in that image to produce a clean, sharp photograph. What happens is that the picture is fuzzy, diagonal lines are jagged, and color is blotchy. The pixels are very visible. In order to give yourself some flexibility, I would suggest buying a camera that has the ability to capture at least 2 to 3.3 megapixels per image. With this number of pixels per image, it is possibile to enlarge photographs to either the 5″ × 7″ or the 8″ × 10″ format. If you really want to do professional-quality prints in a very large format, there are cameras that are capable of 6, 8, or 10 megapixels per image. However, these are very expensive cameras, and I would think that if you were considering that level of photography, you would not need to be reading this book!

Let's get back to resolution and the ability to control your images. Most cameras will let you set the size (number of pixels or the dimensions) of your images. If you know ahead of time that the photographs of your trip will be sent to the family by e-mail, then you can capture the images with a lower resolution setting such as 640 × 480 (307,200 pixels). The advantage of this is that it uses less space on your memory card and that means that you can take more photographs. It also will make it easier to "upload" and "download" the photographs. What happens when, later that day, you are trying to capture that fabulous sunset as you walk along a deserted beach? This is the moment when you change your camera setting to a higher resolution, like 1280 × 960 or 1600 × 1200, which is 1.228 megapixels or 1.92 megapixels respectively. Either one will produce an excellent 5″ × 7″ print and a very good 8″ × 10″ print.

The only considerations here are how much space you have on your memory card, and whether you can use high-speed Internet lines to send out the images. I might note here that the type of camera I use allows me to create two different image sizes for each photograph that I shoot. One produces a high-resolution image that is placed in its own file, usually a JPEG file where each image is about 450 kilobytes, or more, in size. The other is a low-resolution image that is approximately 14 to 16 kilobytes in size. When I look in the folder on my computer for these particular images, I have two separate files—one with the high-resolution images and one with the low-resolution images. I decide whether I am printing or e-mailing the images and pick the correct size for my needs. Then I can decide which ones I might want to edit.

Other Stuff

As far as I am concerned, resolution, pixels, and formats are the most important concepts that you will need to know in order to buy a digital camera or to use it effectively during the first week it is in your possession. There are many other aspects of photography that you might want to learn about later. These include how to adjust the different controls on your camera, such as white balance, sharpness, exposure controls, the different flash features, red-eye, zoom control, etc. Some other things that are important for taking that perfect photograph are composition, lens distortion, perspective, the sun, your position when taking the photograph, and so on.

So why am I stopping here instead of telling you about all these things? There are two reasons. The first is that each camera is different. That is why the owner's manual was invented. Each camera has automatic settings that are its "default settings." When you are just getting started, it is probably best to see what your camera can do without you changing everything around. Once you have taken a lot of photographs and understand the base settings of your camera, then it is time to make adjustments. Maybe you have noticed that certain shots produce a blurred image or one that is always too bright. Maybe a person standing in front of a window on a bright day comes out looking like a dark blob. All these things can be corrected—many within the camera itself, and the rest, to a certain extent, through editing. The key here is to check your LCD screen to get an idea of whether you have taken a good photograph and then to understand that the real image will be seen best on your computer.

At this point I feel that the most important thing for you to do is to get experience with your camera. The more photographs you can take (especially before your trip or special event) the better. (See **Note**, below.) The second reason for moving on to the next stage is that this is not a book on how to take the perfect photograph. This book is meant to teach you what to do after you have taken your photograph. If, in fact, all of your photographs are perfect, then you will not need to read the rest of this book. However, most of us want to make some changes and edit our work, even if it is just to change the shape of the image. With that in mind, let's assume that the photos have been taken, and now we want to get them out of the camera and onto the computer, and to work on "creating" the photograph that we wanted to take in the first place.

Note: The old saying "garbage in, garbage out" applies here to some extent. The digital photography editing process is rather amazing in the number of ways that an image can be modified. At the same time, the computer cannot work miracles. Try to take the best photograph that you can—you will save yourself a lot of trouble when it comes time to using the editing tools. Check your images as you go along and make necessary adjustments using your camera's white balance, sharpness, flash, red-eye reduction, and focus features. The most important thing I can tell you is that *if you have taken a photograph that is not good, delete it right away.* The advantage of digital photography is that you can retake photographs over and over until you get the one that you want. Remember, you are not wasting film and developing costs. Also, depending on the resolution in which you choose to photograph and the size of your memory card, you can return from a one-week vacation with well over 300 photographs. If half of them are not good:

- You will have used up valuable space on your memory card.

- You will have a long and difficult time viewing so many images.
- You will find the whole process daunting and your digital images will soon be like all the loose photographs in your basement that you keep meaning to put into albums "when you have some free time."

3

Chapter 3

Transferring Images (the Key Issue Right Now), Memory (We All Want More, Right?), and More Basics (What You Can Do Without Spending More Money)

We now discuss one of the most important parts of digital photography. In this chapter you will learn how to transfer your photographs to your computer. After all, what good are they if they are still sitting in your camera? In addition, you will learn some of the basic things you can already do with these images, even before working with the editing programs discussed in later chapters.

The operating system of almost every computer includes at least one basic program that will allow you to view your photographs. This program will also let you make some very simple changes. Depending on the camera system you have chosen, a proprietary program for image editing also may have been included on the software CDs that came with your camera. (You now see why I told you to keep all these extra things in a safe place.) Most of these programs, however, are basic, and you will not be able to make too many changes to your image. But they will enable you to have your photographs in a viewable format on your computer. It may not be perfect, but it is a more accurate image than the one you first saw on the LCD screen.

Memory

I have already discussed the fact that there are several types of memory cards on which to store the digital information captured by your camera. However, I want to mention this again because the way you transfer images to your computer will depend on the memory card you are using. Each type of card has advantages and disadvantages. For example, some cameras use floppy disks (or CDs). These are easy to find and inexpensive. They can also go right into your computer without extra hardware. However, floppy disks do not hold a lot of information (so you will need to carry a lot of them), they take a long time to capture each image (meaning the time it takes to shoot the image and then record it on the disk), and they do not take very good high-resolution photographs because of their limited data storage space.

By the way, if you are still taking photographs using 35-millimeter film, you might want to have your images put directly onto a CD (most photo-processing services now offer this option), transfer the images onto your computer, and then edit them with one of the programs I will discuss later.

Sony cameras use a Memory Stick. One of the great advantages of the Memory Stick is that it holds a lot of memory (up to 128 MG) and it fits into all the other Sony devices. This means that you can take your Memory Stick and place it right into your laptop computer to download your photographs.

Another type of memory card is the SmartMedia card. This is a bit of a hybrid. It is relatively small and hold up to 64 MG of information. Its small size means it can fit into smaller cameras. The cards are actually easy to read because they fit into a special floppy disk that also goes right into the computer. The problem is that they can be easily damaged because of their construction, and while they can hold many photographs in smaller resolutions and "lossy" formats, they can only hold a few high-resolution images.

Finally there is the CompactFlash system. Many considered this one of the best systems because of the amount of data that can be placed on one card. With the use of a special adaptor, which is compatible with many cameras, this system is capable of holding up to 1 gigabyte of data, and it is quite small. The advantage here is that with one card you can hold an incredible number of high-resolution images.

While they have different features and capacities, all cards do the same thing, which is to store information of some kind. (Personally I use Sony Memory Sticks, because I use other Sony products, and these Memory Sticks will also hold e-books, music, videos, and many of the chapters I am writing for this book.) Aside from the different speeds used to record data for each type of card, the other factor for you to think about is how to get your information into your computer.

Transferring Photographs from the Camera to the Computer the Basic Way

If you use a memory card that is a CD, floppy disc, or fits into a floppy disk, then you can skip the next few sections and move ahead to the section on creating folders, organizing your images, and viewing your photographs (page 32). Otherwise please read the following paragraphs.

Cables

Remember all the "other things" that came with your camera? There were chargers, memory cards, batteries, etc. Of all of these things, the most important items for you to find right now are the cables and the software (CDs). If you have not loaded the CDs onto your computer yet, do it now. (Open the CD driver, place the CD into the holder, close the holder, and watch as the information for downloading the program appears on your desktop. If it does not, read your owner's manual.) Then attach one end of the cable to the computer and the other end to your camera.

Now here is the question/problem: Do you have a serial cable connection or a USB connection? If you have a serial connection, you will need to go to the back of your computer tower and find the serial port, which, hopefully, is not being used by other equipment. If it is, you will need to disconnect the first cable, turn off your computer, connect the new cable, and restart the computer. If possible, attach your power adaptor to the camera so as not to use up the battery too quickly. If you have a cable with a USB connection, all you have to do is connect the cable to a USB port and to the camera. Now you are ready to transfer your photographs.

As you can see, a serial cable connection is a lot more complicated, and therefore it can have more problems. In addition it is a much slower form of data transfer. One of the problems you might have with this type of connection is that the computer might not "see" it. Sometimes it is a question of recognizing the correct port (you can always try switching to your other serial port), and sometimes there may be another program that is still running that port. For example, I keep the HotSync® cradle for my PDA attached to my serial port, so I would need to disable the HotSync manager if I wanted to use this port for a camera cable. If all else fails, either reinstall your software or call tech support.

With the USB cable, there are very few (if any) problems, and an advantage of this type of connection is that data is transferred at a faster speed. If you do not have a free USB port, all you have to do is take out the device that is using the port and plug in your camera cable. Nothing has to be turned on or off, and nothing has to be "recognized" by the computer.

The downside of using a cable system is that downloading your photographs will still be relatively slow, no matter which type of port connection you use. In addition, unless things change between the time I write this chapter and the time this book appears at your local bookstore or library, the majority of owner's manuals will not tell you how to actually transfer your images from the camera to your computer. This means using common sense and some guesswork. My problem is that each type of camera software is different, so aside from telling you to go to the playback control on your camera, it is hard for me to give you any other directions except this: If you have a problem, call tech support.

Other Transfer Devices

What I will now recommend means spending a bit more money, but it is what most of us use to transfer digital images, and it will save you time and your sanity. Buy a memory-card reader or adaptor that will fit your type of memory card. It is that simple. The reader or adaptor plugs into the USB port on your computer. All you have to do is take the memory card out of your camera and slip it into this device. Then double-click on "My Computer." You will see the reader as an additional drive in the window. Double-click on this drive and a new window will appear, with the folders holding your photographs or the photographs themselves. It is quick, it is easy, it does not waste battery power, and it will place your images on the computer, easily. Then you can delete everything on the memory card, so the card is ready to be used again immediately. After buying a camera, the memory cards, and the computer, I think this is your most important investment and probably the least expensive of them all . There are even readers that can read six different memory cards. This item costs less than $50, so even if everyone in your family chooses a different system, you do not have to spend a fortune.

Before the Actual Transfer—Creating Folders

At this point you *think* you are ready to transfer your images, and basically you are right. There is nothing stopping you from opening "My Computer", finding your memory reading device, opening it, and transferring everything—somewhere.

This is an organizational issue, and we each have our own thoughts about where to put our photographs. The computer (if it is a Windows operating system) will want to send everything to a folder called "My Pictures," which is on the C drive, if you are using Windows 95 or 98. Later versions, like Windows Me and XP, will put the images in "My Documents."

In the long run, this might be the perfect place for all your folders to sit. I personally want to have quick access to my most recent photos in order to name each one and edit them sooner rather than later. What I do is to create a folder on my desktop (right-click anywhere on the desktop, click on "New" on the drop-down menu, and click on "Folder"), and I give it an appropriate name like "Trip with Beth and Paul," "June 03—Bamberg," or "Helen—Birthday." (See figure 3.1) There is nothing like a folder just "staring" at you every day to get you to do some editing! Having said this, there is no reason that you cannot do the same thing (creating and naming a folder) within the primary folder named "My Pictures." Just do not forget about it! (See figure 3.2a.)

Figure 3.1

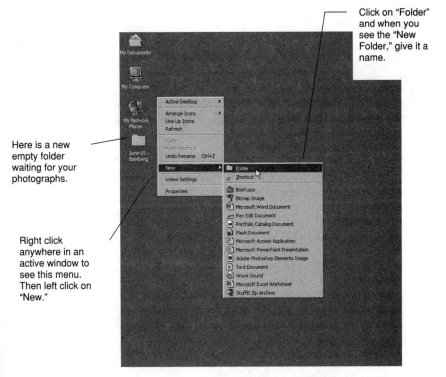

Click on "Folder" and when you see the "New Folder," give it a name.

Here is a new empty folder waiting for your photographs.

Right click anywhere in an active window to see this menu. Then left click on "New."

Follow the same instructions to create a new folder in any active window.

Figure 3.2a

From "My Documents," click
on "My Pictures" to open the
window and create new
folders, or to see the folders
which are already there.

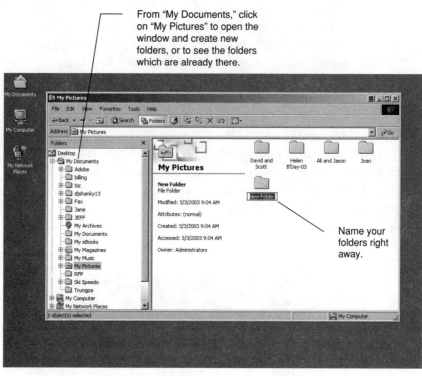

Name your
folders right
away.

So how do you create a folder in "My Pictures"? You need to
double-click on the folder "My Pictures," click on the word
"File" on the menu bar, highlight "New," and click on "Folder."
Then name your new folder. Another way of doing this is to
right-click someplace on the window and first select "New" and
then "Folder." It is easiest if you name the folder immediately,
but if you forget you can always right-click on the folder and
click on "Rename" near the bottom of the drop-down menu. If
you know that you will have several albums at the start of this
process, or if you know that you will put all the photos of David
and Scott in one folder, go ahead and create all of these new
folders at the same time. It does not hurt to be ready ahead of
time. (See figures 3.2a and 3.2b.)

Figure 3.2b

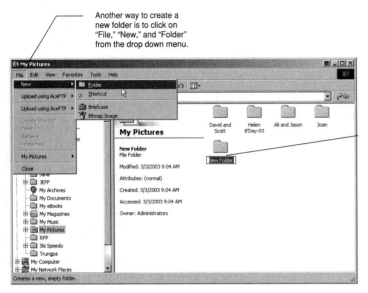

Another way to create a new folder is to click on "File," "New," and "Folder" from the drop down menu.

A new folder will appear and you can type in the name immediately.

Images on Your Computer—The First Viewing

If you are using a basic loading device, you should have a folder with your images on your desktop, or your software may save your photographs to its own program or folder. Your owner's manual should explain how to actually view these images. You will first see these images as icons or in a "thumbnail" size. Again depending on the software that comes with your camera, you should be able to highlight the icon and see a small version of the actual photograph in one corner of the folder window. Double-click on the icon or small thumbnail image to see an enlarged version. There might even be some basic editing tools on a bar on top or to the side of the opened image.

If you are using a memory reader, you first need to go to "My Computer," double-click on the icon, and double-click on

Figure 3.3

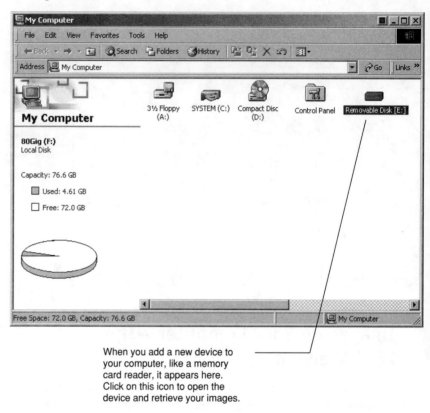

When you add a new device to
your computer, like a memory
card reader, it appears here.
Click on this icon to open the
device and retrieve your images.

the reader. It shows up as a new driver in this folder. The new
window you should see will say something like "Removable
Disk [E:]." (See figure 3.3.) Inside this window there will be at
least one folder, and this is the folder that contains all the images
that came from your memory card. (If there are two folders, it
means you have duplicate images in each, but one is the "e-mail"
size image and the other is our pre-chosen image size. There
may also be a folder with the video images you produced.) Do
not worry, your original images are still on the memory card. If
you play with the original downloaded images and something
gets lost or messed up, you still have all of your photographs
on your memory card. The images will remain there until

you permanently delete them from your memory card. (Later on I make a point of telling you *not* to touch these original downloaded images. *Always* work with copies. You will want to reuse your memory card, so eventually you will delete everything on it to have new storage space and take new pictures.)

Every computer has some kind of photo previewer. Double-click on this folder. In the next window you will probably see a lot of icons, each with funny numbers and letters under it. (See figure 3.4.) This is the way the image software you are using displays and organizes the photographs in this folder. However, this probably does not help you very much. Go to "View" on the menu bar or the view icon on the icon bar (it looks like a box with tiny slides in it) and click on it. You are now given a choice. Among other things, you can view your photographs as icons, or preferably, you can view them as thumbnail images. If possible, change the view to "Thumbnails." You will now see each of your photographs. (If you have an older version of Windows, you might only be able to see your photographs as thumbnail images. This is just

37

Figure 3.4

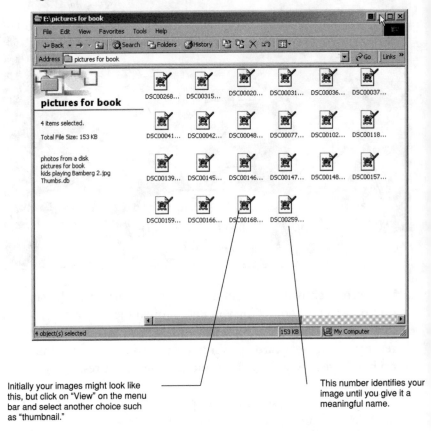

Initially your images might look like this, but click on "View" on the menu bar and select another choice such as "thumbnail."

This number identifies your image until you give it a meaningful name.

fine, as it is really the best way to view them in the beginning. You can check this by going to "Tools" on the menu bar, clicking on it, and then clicking on "Folder Options...." It will tell you if you are using "Classic" or "Web View.")

If you click on a photograph, you will see it on the left side of the window with information as to its size, format, date taken, etc. More importantly, you can now click on "File" on the menu bar and go down to "Rename." Click on this so you can give each photograph a worthwhile label or name. At this point, also be sure to add ".jpg" after each name so that the image

Figure 3.5

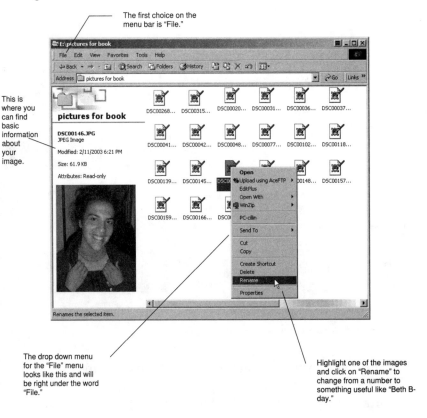

The first choice on the menu bar is "File."

This is where you can find basic information about your image.

The drop down menu for the "File" menu looks like this and will be right under the word "File."

Highlight one of the images and click on "Rename" to change from a number to something useful like "Beth B-day."

format remains the same. Why go to all this trouble right now? It means you won't be trying to figure out what the difference was between DSC00056.jpg and DSC00065.jpg in about ten days' to a month's time. (See figure 3.5.)

Getting back to your images, you now can see them, and you have renamed them. If you are using a later version of Windows, you also have a great advantage, but only for a moment, so do not get too smug. With more recent versions of Windows, you can view your images to the right, and when you highlight an image, it is visible as a larger version in a pane on the left side of the window. Above the window are several icons.

Figure 3.6

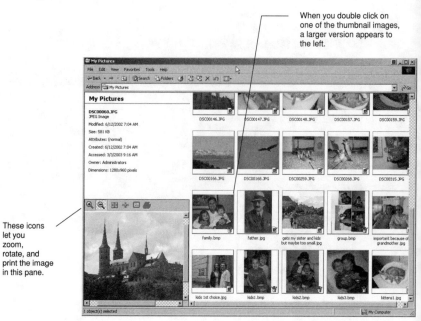

When you double click on one of the thumbnail images, a larger version appears to the left.

These icons let you zoom, rotate, and print the image in this pane.

They will let you zoom in and out, show an even larger image of the photo, rotate the photograph so it is not on its side, and print a copy of it just as it is. (See figure 3.6.)

If you do not have this feature for your first preview window, this is what you do to get it. On the menu bar, click on "View" and then click on "Customize This Folder ... ". The next window is titled "Customize This Folder Wizard." Click the "Next" button. The radio button "Customize" will be selected. Click on the first box "Choose or edit an HTML template for this folder," and click on the "Next" button. (See figures 3.7, 3.8, and 3.9) Now have some fun and click on each of the templates. You can see a preview of each template on the right and a description of each one under the main pane. Click on "Image Preview" and click on the "Next" button. Finally click the "Finish" button.

Figure 3.7

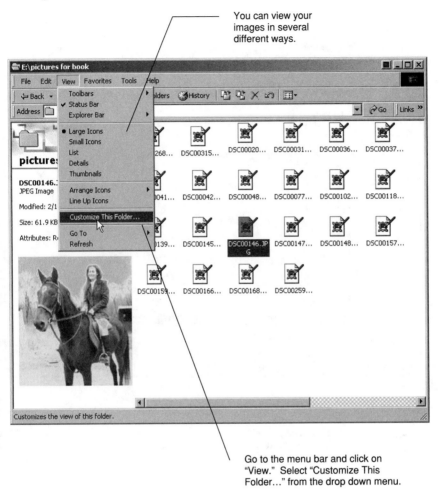

You can view your images in several different ways.

Go to the menu bar and click on "View." Select "Customize This Folder…" from the drop down menu.

Wait just a minute and your original window will change. Now you will have all the same features that are prepackaged in the newer Windows version. You can rotate, zoom, enlarge, and print your photographs.

At this point, if you want to experiment a bit and understand a bit more about pixels and resolution, double-click on one of

Figure 3.8

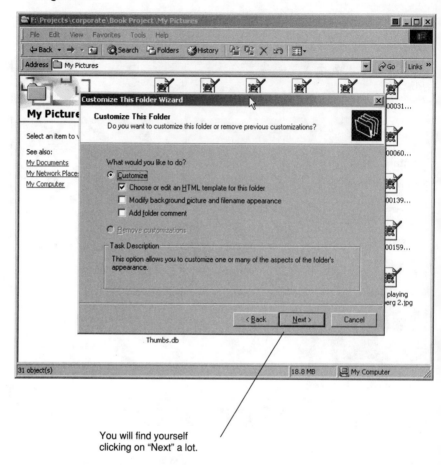

You will find yourself
clicking on "Next" a lot.

your photographs. Next hit the "Zoom in" icon several times,
so that you are really enlarging the photograph.

If your photograph was originally taken at a low resolution,
meaning that it is more the e-mail size of 15 kilobytes and
320 × 240 or 640 × 480 pixels, you will already see a difference
at 150 percent enlargement. At 200 percent enlargement, you
will have a visual demonstration of some of the words that I

Figure 3.9

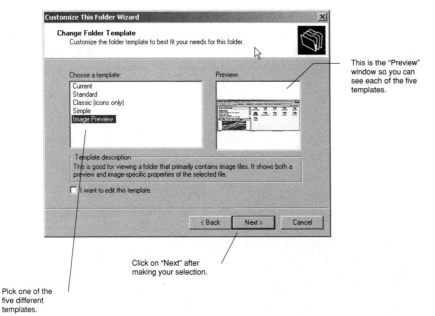

This is the "Preview" window so you can see each of the five templates.

Click on "Next" after making your selection.

Pick one of the five different templates.

used earlier—"jaggies" and "artifacts." What you should notice is that lines (especially diagonal lines) are no longer sharp. These jagged, stair-step lines are known as "jaggies." What has happened is that as the image is enlarged, you now see an area where all the possible squares (pixels) are visible. You also see the software program trying to fill in missing colors in the best way that it can without the extra pixels. This is the blotchy effect called "artifacts." (See figure 3.10.)

So what is the answer to this problem? Well first of all, this is not a problem if you were planning to e-mail these images to the family. Remember, uploading and downloading photographs takes time, and everyone will appreciate the smaller file size. The next thing is that, with luck, you thought about all this ahead of time. That means that you have shot the most important photographs in a higher resolution so that they

Figure 3.10

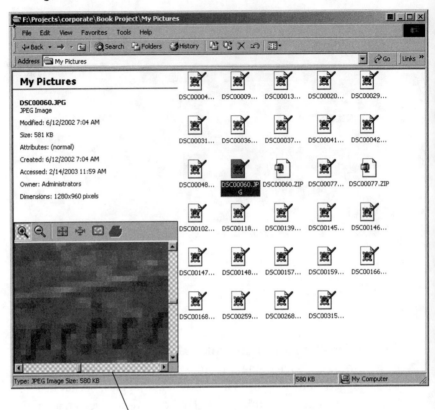

If you enlarge an image too much, all you see are the individual pixels and the programs attempt to fill in what is not there. The blotchy parts are "artifacts."

can be enlarged for printing. Finally, with a nonprofessional camera, there will always be some limit as to how large any image can be enlarged. The bottom line is, be prepared to adjust settings and consider some of the things discussed in the earlier chapters when you take your photographs.

4

Chapter 4
Not All Image-Editing Programs Are Created Equal. However, the Terms You Need to Know Are

All of the things mentioned up to now have been issues concerning the working of the camera, downloading images, organization of images, and basic viewing techniques. In the next few chapters, four of the better image-editing programs will be explained in depth. The reason for covering four programs is that each one has certain advantages and disadvantages. They are all moderately priced. They are easy to use. They all allow you to do the most important editing processes—all the ones that the majority of people will ever need. They also have the additional tools to take you past the basics when you are ready to go further. You will see for yourself which program has the features you need, presented in a way that you find easiest to use. Therefore, after reviewing each of these chapters you can decide which program might work best for you.

Each of the programs that is discussed in the following chapters allows you to edit or change a number of aspects of your picture. Each program is somewhat different from the others, but the basic tools and terms that are used are the same for all of them. For that reason, rather than repeat this information four times, I will use this chapter to explain the meanings of such things as auto fix; contrast and brightness; color, hue, and saturation; rotation; cropping; gamma correction; and more.

As always, I invite you to skip ahead to Chapters 5, 6, 7, and 8 to start working with or reading about the actual programs. However, I do believe you will have a head start in understanding image editing if you know what these words mean and what happens when you use these tools to make changes. Therefore I suggest you read through the next few pages so that you do not have to keep checking the Glossary.

It should be noted that these terms and tools are not listed alphabetically. I think it makes more sense to approach them in the order that they are used for most image editing. In addition, in the following chapters, I will use the names and spelling for each of these items and tools as they appear in the program that I am describing. (Some programs use slightly different terms for the same things.)

In getting started, let's imagine that you have your first photograph on the screen in front of you. If you have held the camera in the primary horizontal position, the orientation of your image will be correct. By this I mean that everyone's heads will be up and the horizon line will run from left to right. If this is not the case, and you turned the camera to take your photograph, the first thing you will want to do is to change the orientation of the image. (To my mind there is nothing more difficult than trying to enhance the sun setting behind some mountains that are lying on their side!)

Rotation

To rotate an image means to move the entire photograph either clockwise or counterclockwise so that it is now oriented the way you would like it to be. Most rotations are made in 90-degree increments. You will see little arrows on the icon bar that show which way you can turn the photograph. However, several programs will allow you to move the image anywhere around a 360-degree circle. Why would you want to do this? Perhaps you are putting together a poster or an invitation, and you want more of a collage look. (My own preference would be to work with an image that is straight up and down, and I would start my general editing this way. You can always play with the little extras later.)

Auto Fix

The auto fix tool is probably the first one that you will want to try once your image is facing the right way. This tool "looks" at the digital image and makes several corrections at the same time. Sometimes this is really all you will need to do. The computer and the editing program agree that these adjustments produce the best image. The auto fix tools in most of the less-expensive programs correct several things at once. However, some programs actually break down the process, so that you can do an auto fix (or "quick fix") for just one level of the entire image at a time, like the brightness and contrast. You can then do minor corrections of this change, or a color correction or saturation correction on your own.

Brightness and Contrast

These tools are grouped together because they affect each other in a complementary way. If you make a change to one, you might also want to change the other at the same time. Having this as a grouped tool just makes editing easier. As you make changes to the "brightness" setting, you see *everything* in an image either lighter or darker. The whole image is modified along the entire spectrum. (See figure 4.1.) "Contrast" is an adjustment between dark and light; it is a manipulation of the two opposites—black and white—while the middle area remains the same. When you increase the contrast, the dark areas get darker in relation to the light areas and the light areas get lighter or whiter in relation to the dark, or black, areas.

Figure 4.1

Brightness Adjustment

Brightness Level Increasing

All pixel values increase equally

Figure 4.2

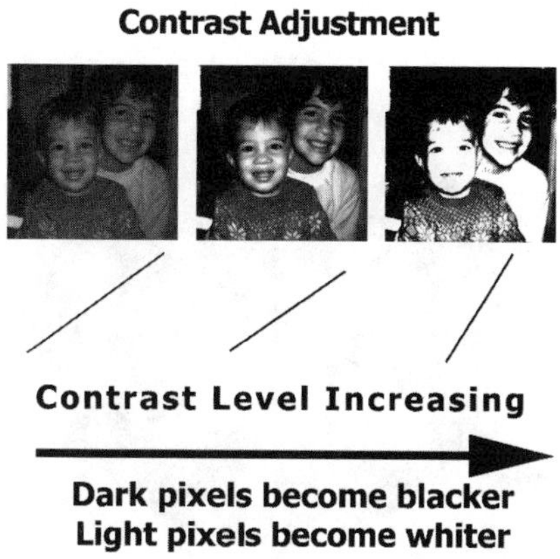

Contrast Adjustment

Contrast Level Increasing

Dark pixels become blacker
Light pixels become whiter

(See figure 4.2.) If the contrast is reduced, you are making dark areas (the pixels) lighter and light areas darker. Increasing contrast makes things look sharper, and decreasing contrast produces a grayer, washed-out image. The key to adjusting brightness and contrast in editing a photograph is to do each of these a little at a time. Go back and forth between the two. Please remember to do things in moderation. If you go to an extreme, you will not be able to remember what you have done a few steps further along, and each change impacts the ones that follow.

Color, Hue, and Saturation

Color refers to two things when editing digital images. If you look at the color wheel, there are the three primary colors—red, green, and blue—and then there are the three opposite or contrasting colors—magenta, yellow, and cyan. Each color has a complementary color. [Another way of stating this is that when the colors overlap they create the shading changes that move you around the color wheel. In moving the "correction" slide or tab, you are actually moving from primary colors to contrasting colors along this color wheel or the color

Figure 4.3

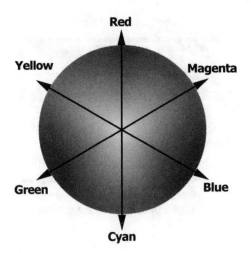

cones.] (See figure 4.3.) The color of an image is changed by either increasing or decreasing the opposite color proportionally, or by changing the two colors that are next to it. Technically another way of looking at this is that if you add all the primary colors together the image will become white, and if you add all the complementary colors together the image will be black. To see things properly on the monitor, you need to adjust the color slide to trade off one for the other.

Hue is color in its purest form, with no black, gray, or white added; it is represented as a specific point on a color wheel. That is because it is a "value" of a color based on transmitted light or reflected light. Hue is adjusted by rotating the point on the color wheel 360 degrees. (See figures 4.4a and 4.4b.) In fact it is a very difficult tool to use as a novice editor, and while it is fun to play with, it should only be used for "fine-tuning" an image. As you change the hue, all the colors are changed. (Obviously, hue is not only difficult to use, but also difficult to describe. The best way for me to think about it is this: When

Figure 4.4a

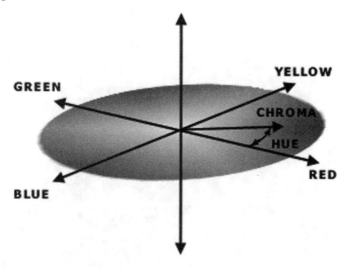

I would see green faces on my old color television set, I knew I had to adjust the hue control.)

Saturation is the intensity of the color, or purity of the hue. It is the amount of hue in relation to gray. The more vibrant the image, the more saturation involved. All of this is measurable on a scale of 0 (gray) to 100 (full saturation).

Gamma Correction

A gamma correction tool is used to adjust the brightness of the middle range (gray tones) of an image. It adjusts the intensity of the light spectrum (colors) to fit the capabilities of the hardware on which an image will be seen, such as the monitor or printer. In other words, if the white and black (light and dark) areas are fine, but the middle range of colors are wrong, a gamma correction will adjust the middle range of brightness to add or reduce color. (See figure 4.5.) In fact if you look at your photograph and think that everything looks pretty good and it

Figure 4.4b

This photo, viewed in color, shows an example of what happens when you go to extremes with the "Hue" correction on an image.

Figure 4.5

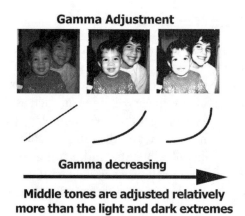

Gamma Adjustment

Gamma decreasing

Middle tones are adjusted relatively more than the light and dark extremes

is just the middle range of colors that are "off," the only editing you might need to do is a gamma correction.

Red-Eye Reduction

"Red eye" is the term used to describe the red light that appears in a photograph. It shows the reflection of the retina in the eye of a person or animal. It is usually caused by the intense light flash of the camera hitting the back of the eye when it is wide open. All editing programs have a way of touching up the area to change the color from red to another color (usually black).

Cropping

To "crop" an image is to change the size and/or shape of the image. Sometimes you will take a photograph and decide that you do not want some of the background in the finished picture. By using the cropping tool, lines are drawn around the part of the image that you want to keep. This section is then saved. It is the digital way of reframing your image. It is the same as taking a pair of scissors and cutting out the part of your image you wished you had never photographed in the first place.

Bonus Information: Sharpen and Blur

A friend just asked me to add this information, so now you do not have to go to the Glossary to look up these definitions. Sharpening an image is sometimes confused with adding contrast to the photograph; initially the overall effect is the same. What is different is that when an image is sharpened, the editing program is bringing out the details of the photograph rather than increasing the difference between dark and light. The pixels are accentuated. Too much sharpening can produce unpleasant results by adding artifacts and jaggies. Blurring the photograph is just the opposite. It blends the pixels to soften the overall effect. In each case it is a question of personal taste or artistic creativity.

So is this all that you can do to edit your photograph? Of course not. Just look at all the additional icons and toolbars in each image-editing program. However, I think that these are the main types of changes you will want to make, especially in the beginning. By all means take a photograph that you do not really care about and play with it. Try the equalization tool. It lets you stretch light or dark areas that have been over- or underexposed. It does this while at the same time evening out all the colors in between. Another thing that is fun to do is to change from the "modern" look of color to a sepia or black-and-white image. Play with the "oil painting," "watercolor," "negative," or "line" editing tools to see some other alternatives. Basically go ahead and have fun, but again I strongly suggest that you do this with one of your "throwaway" images or with a copy. Sometimes you will make so many changes that you will never get back to the original image.

5

Chapter 5
Microsoft® Picture It!®
Version 7.0

Microsoft Picture It! is a very popular program for a number of reasons. It is moderately priced at approximately $55, and it is easy to use with a clear and intuitive "work space." As it is a Microsoft product, it is meant to work well with the different Windows operating systems. However, there are also some disadvantages to this program, and I will point them out at the end of this chapter. In that way you have a chance to play with this program a bit without prejudging it.

As with all of these image-editing programs, the first thing you will need to do is to load the CD onto your computer and run through the basic installation procedures. Once this is done, open the Picture It! program by clicking on "Start," "Programs," and then "Microsoft Picture It!"

The first window that you will see on the initial start-up is a window that is meant to be a helpful tool to familiarize yourself with the basics of the program. It is called Picture It! Tour. By all means go through all the tutorials in this section if you like, but to my mind, the most useful things to do are:

1. Close this window.
2. Look at the work space in front of you.
3. Find the "Common Tasks" bar, which is a vertical bar on the left side.
4. Click on the last icon, "Startup Window."
5. From this new window, click on "Instructional Videos" (second line down on the left side, under "Help Center.") (See figures 5.1 and 5.2.)

The first instructional video (in blue, halfway down the right pane of the window) is a tour of the "work area." This is probably the only part of the Help Center you need right now. It shows you where everything is on this primary window. It covers such things as how to move the image you want to edit from the "tray" onto the "work space," and what is meant by

Figure 5.1

This is the "Common
Tasks" bar.

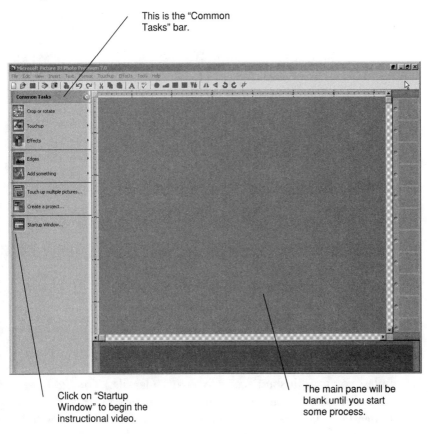

Click on "Startup
Window" to begin the
instructional video.

The main pane will be
blank until you start
some process.

the term "canvas." It also shows you how to access the menu
bar, the toolbar, and the Common Tasks bar.

Your real starting point is to open the "File Browser." You need
to do this to find the file or folder where you are storing the
images that you would like to edit. Go to "File" on the menu
bar and click on "Open." The File Browser window will appear.
(See figure 5.3.) On the left side there is a pane where you can
see a list of all your folders. The one that is highlighted is
"My Pictures," as this is the default image storage space for the

Figure 5.2

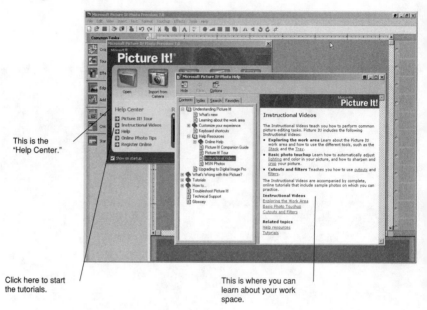

This is the
"Help Center."

Click here to start
the tutorials.

This is where you can
learn about your work
space.

Windows operating systems. (Microsoft considers this the first step in organizing your folders, and it is an easy way to start unless you want instant access to a particular file.) The right pane shows all the files of pictures that you have saved to this folder. Double-click on one of these files, and your images will appear in the "thumbnail" format. (These are small previews of each image. There is a slide bar on top of the right pane that lets you make these bigger if you are having trouble seeing them.)

If you want to work with all of the images in this folder, highlight them all by pressing the "Control" key and the "A" key at the same time (Ctrl + A). Then click on the "Open" button to move all the thumbnail images to the Picture It! tray in the work-space window. Finally, click on the image with which you want to work. (If you only want to move one of the photographs, double-click on that single image.) As a point of

Figure 5.3

To open the "File Browser," click on "File" and then "Open" on the drop down menu

Use the slide bar to make the images larger.

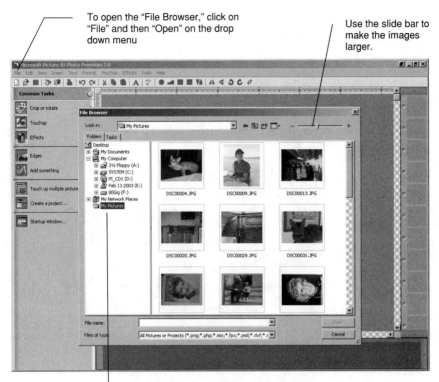

From "File Browser," click on "My Pictures" to see all your folders. Select and click on a folder to see the individual images.

interest, if you stop to look at the work space, the window should now have the name of your image (or the number) on the title bar along with the format such as "JPG." You will also see the name of this photo-editing program. (See figure 5.4.)

At this point you can see why this program is considered "user-friendly." All the tools you need are on the left side of the window in the area called "Common Tasks." They even are listed in the order in which you probably want to use them. You can also find all of these tools on the menu bar, as sub-menus,

Figure 5.4

The name or number of your image is here along with the name of the program that you are using.

The selected image will fill the main pane.

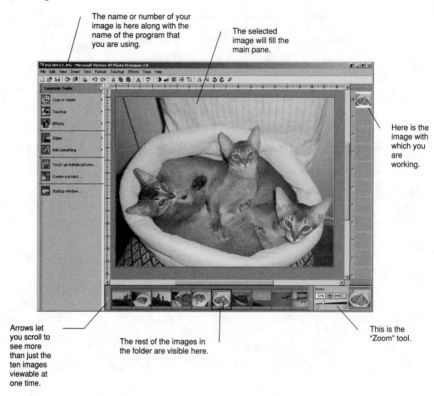

Here is the image with which you are working.

Arrows let you scroll to see more than just the ten images viewable at one time.

The rest of the images in the folder are visible here.

This is the "Zoom" tool.

and on the toolbar, where they are shown as icons. However, using the "Common Tasks" bar is much simpler and will probably cover all of your needs. Another thing to notice is the "zoom finder" on the bottom right of the primary pane. This appears in each of the views. It is a useful tool that lets you see exactly what area you are working with. It is important to understand, however, that zooming in or out will not affect the printed size of the image. It is merely a tool to help you see things more clearly. There is also a useful bar to the right of the primary pane that can hold a number of images. It is useful if you want to layer one image over another. This is an example of

Figure 5.5

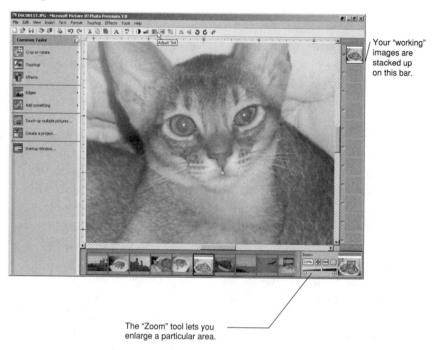

Your "working" images are stacked up on this bar.

The "Zoom" tool lets you enlarge a particular area.

the kind of thing that you would want to use to make a collage. (See figure 5.5.)

Crop and Rotate

The first task on the bar is "Crop or rotate." Rotate is first on the list of tasks, and this is always my first choice. If you click on this tool, you can turn your image left or right 90 degrees, upside down (180-degree rotation), or customize the angle to any compass heading you would like. Each one of these options is previewed under the button for the particular command. There is a "Reset" button and also a "Help" button. If you like what you see, just click on the "Done" button. If not, click on the "Cancel" button to wipe out everything and start over with something else. (On the menu bar, you can find the command for rotate under "Format," and on the toolbar this icon is shown as two curved arrows that are second from the right just before the icon for cropping. However, there is a difference between the two. If you click on the menu bar version, it gives you the same view as the "Common Tasks bar." The icon for rotation simply does the task.)

The next choice is whether to crop your photograph. This is something you may or may not wish to do. If you do want to cut out unwanted parts of the image or reshape it, click on the second choice. It is just below "Rotate." Your new window will show the image in the main pane on the right, but you will notice that it is not as bright as the original. On the left you have several choices. My suggestion is to start by clicking the down arrow next to the word "Custom" and choosing a traditional-size print—such as 5″ × 7″. This way you can work with a standard that is mistake-proof for later printing. (If you want a custom-sized image go to the next step, right below the main box. Here you can decide the exact size of the crop.) You can also see that there are a number of fancy shapes available to you that might be fun to use when creating something for a special event. An example might be the clover leaf shape for a St. Patrick's Day card. (See figures 5.6a and 5.6b.)

Once you have set the size (or shape) you want, place the cursor at the spot where you want to begin the crop. This is where the first "side" of the finished image will start. Next hold down the left mouse button while dragging the cursor to the right. When you have your complete image outlined, release the left mouse button. Notice that the area you enclosed is now bright again, and it appears to be in a white frame.

There are orange dots around the cropped image. These can be used to change the shape of the image. (Note that doing this will change the printable image.) The dots in the middle of each side are for non-proportional changes such as stretching the image

Figure 5.6a

There are many shapes to choose from when you want to crop an image. You do not have to just make the crop rectangular.

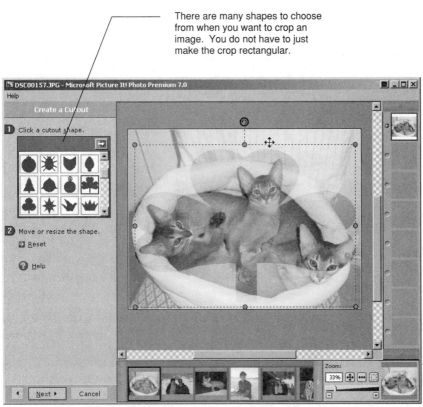

in different directions. (Do this by holding down the "Control" [Ctrl] key while moving the buttons.) The other thing you can do is to change the new image from vertical to horizontal (or anything in between) by clicking and holding down the "Rotate" button at the top of the crop box. Go ahead and have some fun with your image. Hold down the left mouse button and make circles with the "Rotate" button! (See figure 5.7.)

If you decide that "the size is right," but you really would like to have a different portion of your photograph as your finished image, put the cursor in the middle of the crop area, hold down the left mouse button, and move the actual crop box to another

Figure 5.6b

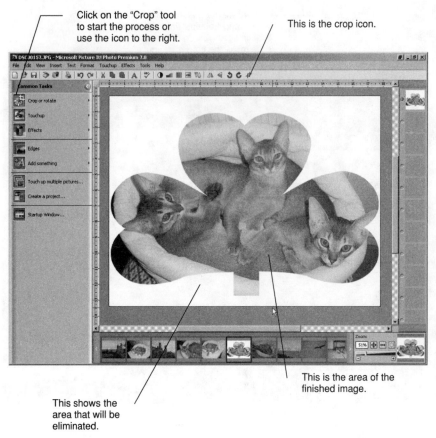

Click on the "Crop" tool to start the process or use the icon to the right.

This is the crop icon.

This is the area of the finished image.

This shows the area that will be eliminated.

location. This way you can include part of that snow-covered tree in the left corner, while keeping the people you want to see on the right. As always, when you are happy with the new image click on the "Done" button, or click on the "Cancel" button and start all over again.

Touchup

The next tool that you are offered is "Touchup." This allows you to change the brightness and contrast, adjust the tint (colors),

Figure 5.7

This is the Rotate button.

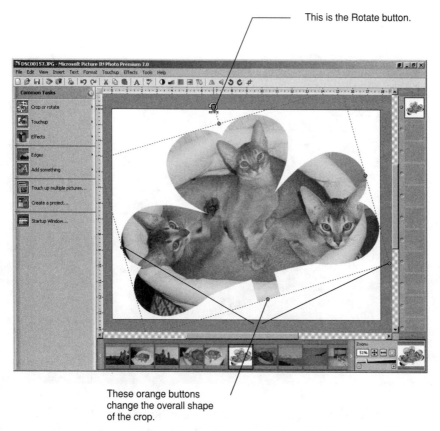

These orange buttons
change the overall shape
of the crop.

fix red eye, and sharpen or blur your image. Best of all, the first
choice you have in this category is "Contrast Auto Fix" "Levels
Auto Fix." Click on the "Levels Auto Fix" button and you will
immediately see what the program thinks you ought to do to
improve your photograph. This is always a good way to start,
because if you like the changes, you are finished with that part
of the edit. (See figures 5.8a and 5.8b.)

Brightness and Contrast

If you want a little more control over your image, click on
"Brightness and Contrast." This window gives you just a few

Figure 5.8a

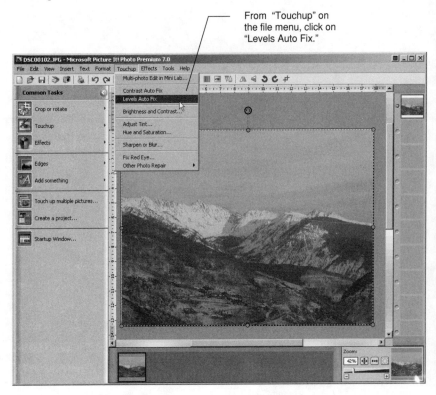

From "Touchup" on
the file menu, click on
"Levels Auto Fix."

more options. Again you can go for the "Levels auto fix" and/or
the "Contrast auto fix." Then you can make some of your own
adjustments, using the slide buttons that are just below. Of
course there are always the "Reset" button to take you back to
your original image, and a "Help" button to explain in detail
some of the things that I have not already mentioned. If all of
this is not what you want to do right now, click on the "Cancel"
button. If you *do* like the results, click on the "Done" button.
(See figure 5.9.)

Tint or Color

Your next choice is to "Adjust Tint." This is a tool that shows
color that is added or subtracted. You are taking color and

Figure 5.8b

The alternative is to click on "Touchup" on the "Common Tasks" bar and then click on "Levels auto fix" from the drop down menu.

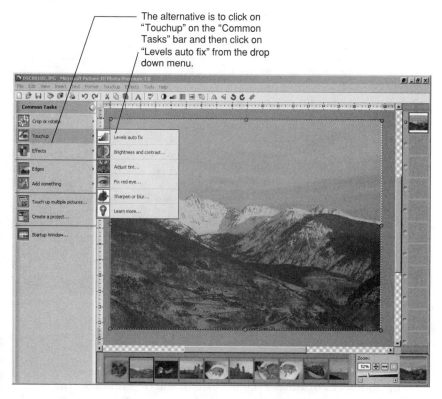

adjusting it to a new part of the whole palette of colors. It is needed because all the colors in the image may be "off" because of an incorrect "white balance." Again there is a button that will do an auto fix. However, you also have an interesting tool that allows you to correct the "white balance." This is something that is important because you may not have considered it (an oversight, of course) when you took the original photograph. (See figures 5.10 and 5.11.)

This brings up a whole new topic that is worth discussing here. Every type of light gives off its own special color, so the concept of the color "white" is not a fixed thing. Depending on whether you are taking a picture in sunlight or in a room with

Figure 5.9

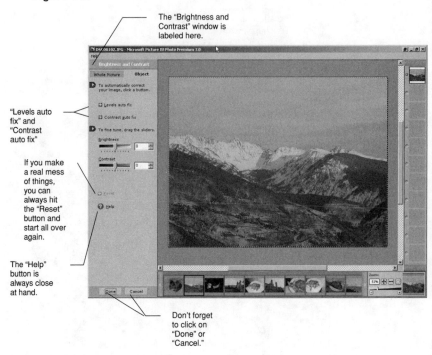

The "Brightness and Contrast" window is labeled here.

"Levels auto fix" and "Contrast auto fix"

If you make a real mess of things, you can always hit the "Reset" button and start all over again.

The "Help" button is always close at hand.

Don't forget to click on "Done" or "Cancel."

incandescent or tungsten lights, there will be a different tint to an object that you know should be white. It will be bluer in incandescent light, and it will have a yellowish tint in sunlight. (This should not surprise you. If you think about it, the brand of 35-millimeter film that you used before getting your digital camera also had a "bias" that produced photographs with different color tints. That is why some people use one brand when taking outdoor photographs at the beach and a different brand when shooting indoor events.)

In Picture It! the cursor looks like an eyedropper when it is placed over the image. Place the cursor (eyedropper) over a spot that you know should be white and then click once. The program will then correct the white and all the other colors. Another way of doing this is to click the dropper in lots of

Figure 5.10

The eyedropper can be moved around with the mouse just like a cursor.

There are several ways to correct the white balance.

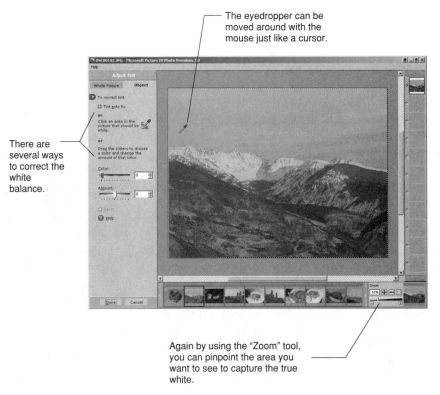

Again by using the "Zoom" tool, you can pinpoint the area you want to see to capture the true white.

different areas just to experiment and to see if the result is something that you find pleasing.

However, the results are often suspect, because the program cannot judge the colors in the image as you can. That is why there are two slide buttons two-thirds of the way down this pane. They allow you to make your own color corrections. Color correction goes through a rainbow, and the slide bar actually shows the amount of color that is physically added or subtracted from the picture. (See figure 5.11.) When you want to stop fooling around or need to start over, click on the "Reset" button, the "Cancel" button to forget about the whole thing, or

Figure 5.11

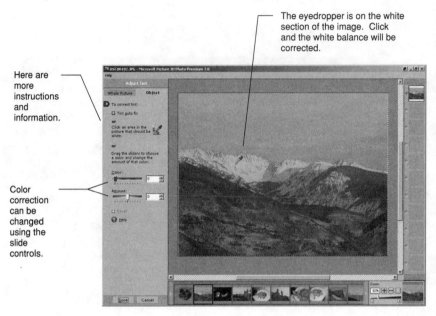

The eyedropper is on the white section of the image. Click and the white balance will be corrected.

Here are more instructions and information.

Color correction can be changed using the slide controls.

"Done" if you like your results. More importantly, if you do not think I have explained all this clearly enough, click on "Help."

Red Eye

"Fix Red Eye" is your next adjustment, if this is a problem with your image. The first step is to use the zoom tool to isolate the eye or eyes that are a problem. Click on the red section of each eye. Then click on the "Red-eye auto fix" button. If this does not work properly, you can always reset to the original image and try it again.

Sharpen or Blur

This tool uses a simple slide button to change the settings. The one caution here is that while it might be nice to soften an image, you need to be careful before sharpening the photo too much. "Sharpen" can bring out details, but the actual print might wind up having a lot of "artifacts" and "jaggies." There is no set formula for this one. You need to play with it and have an artistic eye.

General Thoughts about Picture It!

I have already talked about the advantages of this program. It is easy to use and inexpensive. Everything is well placed, and the directions for each adjustment are clear. There are half a dozen special effects, a variety of borders, and you can add text to your images. There is a special section near the end of the "Common Tasks" bar that offers many projects that are easy to construct with dozens of templates. You can even edit multiple images at the same time. This is a big help when you want to rotate 25 images that are all 90 degrees to the left!

So what are the disadvantages of this program? One of the things that I do not like is that on the "work space" or canvas, you only see the changes that are currently being made to your photograph. You do not know what the baseline is. Something was done to your photograph, and you do not know exactly what it was. By that I mean that there is no way of comparing the "before" and "after" unless you can jump from the "Reset" button to your correction very quickly. (In order to remember the changes made, you might want to have a notepad on your desk or by your side. This way you can jot down the position or numbers shown to the side of the slide control as you go along.)

I am also concerned about the fact that once you click on "Done," there is no way of going back to your original image. For each individual change, you can click on the "Undo" button, but you are only taken back one "move." There is also the "Reset" button to take you back to the beginning, or the "Cancel" button to end that particular adjustment. However, all this is moot once you decide to commit to the adjusted image by clicking the "Done" button and closing the window.

The same is true when you use the auto fix tool repeatedly. The thing to remember here is that each level is cumulative, and this can get tricky. (Repeated "auto fix" clicking can make some strange changes to the image.) Try to remember always to go back to the original image by clicking on the "Reset" button before working with individual controls. This is the purest form of digital information you have, and an auto fix may have lost something. (**Note**: This is another reason for making a copy of your photograph and working only with this copy. If all else fails, you will always have the original intact.)

Finally, this is a program where it is important to follow *its* order of tasks when making your changes. Each "fix" affects the other changes that you have made. The results of adjusting contrast first and then tint will be different than changing the tint and then the contrast.

6

Chapter 6
Jasc® After Shot™ Premium Edition

Jasc Software™ is a company that has created some wonderful image-editing programs for the professional or "high end" user. These are the people who need to have advanced programs for artwork production, etc. After Shot Premium Edition is the company's first image-editing program for the individual who wants to do basic photographic editing, with some added features for special projects. There are a number of excellent features in this program that are carryovers from the more advanced programs made by this company. In addition, its moderate price (roughly $50) makes it an attractive choice.

Jasc has released an updated version of the program After Shot that is called Paint Shop Photo Album. Many of the features described in this chapter are the same as the features in the new program. For this reason, you will have no difficulty using whichever program you decide to buy. The added special features of the updated version of this program are included at the end of this chapter.

One of the best features of this image-editing program is that it emphasizes one of the key aspects of digital photography—the organization of your photographs into easily accessible folders. A box of 35-millimeter prints labeled "kittens 1996–2003" or "Joan—school" may have been your best form of cataloging to date, but if you try this system on your computer, it will be a disaster. After Shot also gives you an easy way to label or name your photos, and you can do this both individually and in batches. This is a great time-saver. There are several other things that I really like about this program, but let's run through the basics and you will see for yourself.

As with all software, in order to begin the program After Shot you must first load the CD that came with the user guide, registration forms, and free offers. The first screen you will see will offer a number of choices of programs to download. If all you are planning to do is image editing, just install After Shot. (Acrobat® Reader™ is for reading the manual, and I personally

prefer to do this by turning the pages of a real book. QuickTime™ is for viewing slide shows and movies.) You will see all the usual windows, so follow the directions. This means you will click on "Next" several times, "Yes" at least once, and fill in all the personal information requested. Now this is important: You will be asked if you want to use After Shot as your "default" editing program. Think about this and consider reading about the other programs discussed in this book before making this selection. It is something that can always be changed, and it is just as easy to go to the "Start" menu and choose it from the list of programs. Register online and then click on "Finish."

Now at this point two things happen that I consider annoying. The initial window appears again to check whether you want to consider installing any of the programs that you neglected to select the first time around. The other thing is that there will now be an icon of a camera on the task tray. This is the "Cameo Viewer" for use with your camera. (The "Cameo Viewer" helps you to see your images and download them. It also helps to launch this particular program. Your images appear in a vertical strip on the right side of your desktop.) Anyway, I do not think you need it right now so remove it from the tray.

When this is all done, click on "Start," click on "Programs," go to "Jasc Software," and click on "Jasc After Shot 1." The first thing you will see (briefly) is the main window and then the "Quick Tour" window. This is actually one of the better informational tours available. The "Getting Started" section shows many of the buttons and what they do. The "Catalog & Search" tour explains the organization of photographs clearly and simply. The "Editing Images" tour is like a Microsoft® PowerPoint presentation that takes you through many of the editing tools that are discussed in the rest of this chapter. I think you will find it most useful to view the "Quick Tour," read my directions for editing, and then refer back to the "Editing Images" section if there is something that is unclear. All the other tours and the projects they describe will be fun to play with later.

The main window for After Shot has the usual menu bar and toolbar. The toolbar has a number of very useful icons for quickly getting to special tasks. One of my favorite tools is "Batch." It allows you to take a whole group of images and rename all of them at once, or rotate them, or do a quick fix on the lot. However, let me warn you: **The disadvantage of "Batch" is that there is no "Undo" command.** That is why I would only use this for renaming and rotating *selected* photographs.

On the left side of the window you will see a list of files and folders from the "Browser" tab (the first selected tab). Select a folder and the primary pane will be filled with the images that you have chosen to view. This is a normal file browser, much like the one you are used to using from the Windows Explorer menu. Among the other tabs is "Info," which provides the album name, additional title, and description. It also lists other information that has been saved with the images, such as date, type, size, bits for color, things the camera did with speedsettings and other settings, etc. This is a good place to rename your folder with a title that might be more useful. The "Keywords" and "Search" tabs are for organizational data—who, what, when, what size, whatever. (See figures 6.1a and 6.1b.)

Going back to the "Browse" tab, you are most likely to find your photographs in "My Documents" under "My Pictures". This is the default for this program. When I look in this folder, I find several folders to choose from, but for this exercise I suggest

Figure 6.1a

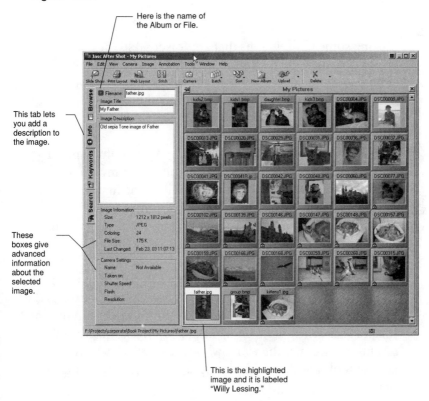

Here is the name of the Album or File.

This tab lets you add a description to the image.

These boxes give advanced information about the selected image.

This is the highlighted image and it is labeled "Willy Lessing."

Figure 6.1b

The "Browser" tab shows the folders.

The "Keywords" and "Search" tabs will make organization easier.

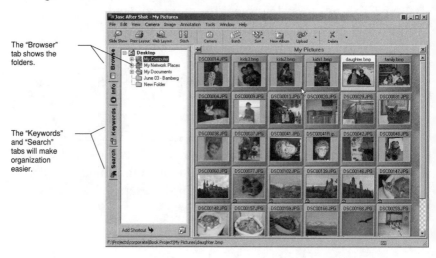

picking some photographs that are "disposable" or that are copies of the original. (**Note:** I must emphasize again that you should always make copies of your images and do all your editing on the copies. In that way if something goes drastically wrong, you have saved the original.)

I am going to work on a general grouping of photographs. By clicking on this folder, I now have 30 photos of my wonderful children at different ages and my "family". The first view is in the "thumbnail" format. In order to start my editing, I double-click on one of the images. That is the easiest way of starting. (See figure 6.1a.)

The next window is my editing window. To the left of the main pane are all the photographs in this folder. On the bottom is the name and location of this folder. If I want to work with several images and switch between them quickly, these images will also be at the bottom of the window. (More on this later.) All of the editing tools are above the photograph on the new toolbar. (See figure 6.2)

Figure 6.2

Click here to "Rotate" the image.

I used a little "Zoom" for this image. Note the button is depressed.

After selecting an image, you can see the editing tool bar.

You can find the name of the image and its location here.

Rotate

As you should know by now, I think that it is best to view a photograph in the correct orientation. Therefore I always rotate the image first. The icon for rotation is on the toolbar, the third from the left. You have the choice of clicking on the word "Rotate," which will automatically turn the image 90 degrees with each click, or you can click on the down arrow just to the right of the icon. If you do the latter there are several options. The reason for this is that you might want to do an "Exact . . . " or "Free" rotation. This is not just to make some fancy image for a leaflet, but is useful for those times when you may have tilted the camera off center while taking the photo. This allows you to correct this mistake without the whole world knowing that you cannot line up a shot of a sunset while hanging over the railing of a sailboat. Another way of doing a rotation is to go to the menu bar, click on "Image," highlight "Rotate," and click on the direction you want to turn the image.

Crop and Resize

In order to do a crop, click on the fourth icon from the left on the toolbar. To use the menu bar, you need to click on "Image" and select "Crop." Please note that After Shot offers several interesting options for reshaping your photograph. That is why the heading of this section is "Crop and Resize." There is the straightforward approach of cropping, which is to select your image and then click on the icon (which looks like different sizes of paper) to the bottom right of the image. A drop-down menu allows you to select the standard size image that you want, or it offers a "freehand" approach for selecting the size of the image you want to save. (See figure 6.3.)

If you pick a standard size such as 4″ × 6″, the white crop box will adjust to that size and actually "remember" this as your main choice for future crops. (This is not set in stone, and you can always change the size, but it will default to this original size first.) As with most programs, once you have picked the size of your image, you can move the whole box around to capture the exact area you want to save. For the moment, notice that there is a box in the middle of this lower bar that gives you a set of numbers (more on these in a moment). Finally there is another icon on the lower right that allows you to arrange the 4″ × 6″ image as a portrait (vertical) or landscape (horizontal) print. (See figure 6.4a)

Now, I do not recommend getting into this next section (resizing), because I think it falls under the category of "the second week with my new digital camera." However, the reason

Figure 6.3

Clicking on "Image" from the menu bar lets you see the drop down menu. It includes "Crop" and "Rotate." You can also use the icons for this.

for mentioning the numbers on the lower bar of the crop window is that you can also resize your photograph based on the number of pixels that you want in your printed image. This gets a bit complicated as most of us have no idea how many pixels we might want to use. (See Appendix B for more information on this.)

If you do want to play with this, the program makes it a little easier for you by offering the option of keeping the "aspect ratio" of the image. This means that if you decide on a $4'' \times 6''$ image, as you change the number for the width, the height will change proportionally. Try this out by pointing the cursor on

81

Figure 6.4a

Move this box to position the exact area you want for your crop.

This tool "grabs" the crop box and lets you move it around.

This is the image you will see after the crop.

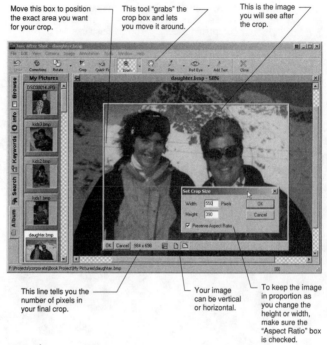

This line tells you the number of pixels in your final crop.

Your image can be vertical or horizontal.

To keep the image in proportion as you change the height or width, make sure the "Aspect Ratio" box is checked.

Figure 6.4b

By moving the crop box around, I now have just the image of my daughter.

This is the area that will be lost when I complete the crop.

82

Figure 6.4c

The finished crop

The original image

the numbers in the box. First they will turn blue, and then if you click once, a new box will appear, "Set Crop Size." You can play with the numbers and see what happens. (See figures 6.4a, 6.4b, and 6.4c.)

The correct way to actually resize the image is to click on "Image" on the menu bar, select "Resize . . . ," and work with a new window. (See figure 6.5.) This one will not show you your image, but will show you the shape that your image will have as you change the number of pixels. Why is all this important? If you have already played with the "Zoom" tool, you know that you can increase or decrease the photograph so that you can check individual details. (The left mouse button increases the size and the right decreases it. The little arrow to the right of the "Zoom" button lets you pick a certain percentage without all the zooming in and out.)

Figure 6.5

Select "Image" from
the menu bar and click
on "Resize."

This window shows the
actual shape of your
resized image along with
the number of pixels.

However, zooming *magnifies*; it does not change the actual size
of the image. If you resize the image, it means that when you
enlarge the photograph, the program calculates the additional
pixels required to "fill in" the spaces that are empty. This means
that the new, bigger, image might be blurred, as the program
can only guess as to the color and position of pixels. If you
shrink the image, then the new calculations have to figure out
how to squeeze everything into a much smaller area. This also
can cause a blurred image.

As usual, my suggestion is to take a photograph that you do not
care about and play with all these tools. In fact, have two or

three photographs ready. Unless you remember *always* to click on "Undo" *immediately*, you will get stuck with a very strange image. Having the spare photos will reduce your frustration level and train you to click "Undo" after each of your changes unless you really love what you have created.

Quick Fix

The icon for this tool is the fifth one from the left on the toolbar, or you can find it on the menu bar as the first choice under "Image." As with Microsoft Picture It!, this is always a good place to begin. If you want to try making your own changes, be sure to click on the "Undo" icon (first on left) before continuing. This program only has one level of "Undo," and if you continue with changes, you will not be able to go back to the beginning. (Just watch the arrow flip back and forth a few times and you will understand.) Now if you like the new image, terrific. However, for this exercise I would like you to look

85

carefully at the Quick Fix of this program, then cancel (or undo) this change and move on to the next type of correction.

Corrections

For the program After Shot, all of the basic editing tools are grouped under the heading "Corrections." This includes contrast and brightness, color, hue and saturation, sharpness, and equalization. It is the second icon from the left on the toolbar and can also be found as the second choice under "Image" on the menu bar.

Open this window and I think you will see why I really like this program. (See figure 6.6.) Not only is everything grouped logically, but you can also see the "before and after" of each image on one screen as you make the correction. By moving a slide control there is a vertical separator showing the changes you have made and it allows you to view every portion of the image and of your correction. Why is this important? You might think that the area on the right needs to be brighter. You make the correction and the right side looks great. By moving the slider to the left of center, you can also see if the left side of the image is improved by this change. Maybe you have lightened the entire photograph too much with this correction. Normally you would only know this by checking the different areas separately by going back and forth with corrections. This window lets you do it with a simple click and drag.

There are other things that make this an "elegant" and useful window. The first is that you can move back and forth between the different tabs, and you do not need to "Save" your image until everything is done. I think this is a wonderful place to *really* see what it means to change colors and pigments, hue and saturation, and brightness and contrast.

The sliders for each of these corrections actually label what happens when you move to the right and left. An added feature

Figure 6.6

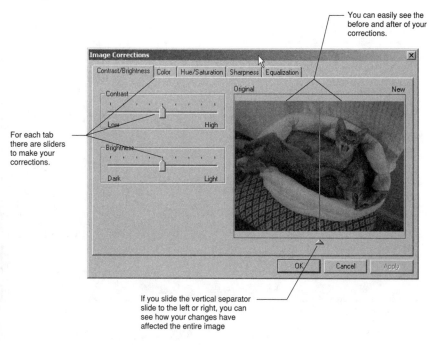

You can easily see the before and after of your corrections.

For each tab there are sliders to make your corrections.

If you slide the vertical separator slide to the left or right, you can see how your changes have affected the entire image

lets you change "brightness" not only with contrast but also with hue and saturation. This is important because when you change the saturation, you often have to change the brightness level. In addition, using this program is a great way to actually see what I have been talking about when I say that excessive sharpening of an image will bring out the jaggies and artifacts. (See figure 6.7.)

So having raved about this window and its features, let me mention some of the negatives. It is very tempting to play with color, hue, and saturation, especially when it appears that each of these edits are so well-defined. The fact is that they are still very tricky. Unless you have created a problem because you did not consider lighting conditions, etc., when you took the photo, they are not things to adjust if you are working on an important photograph. Also, if you make a lot of changes and

Figure 6.7

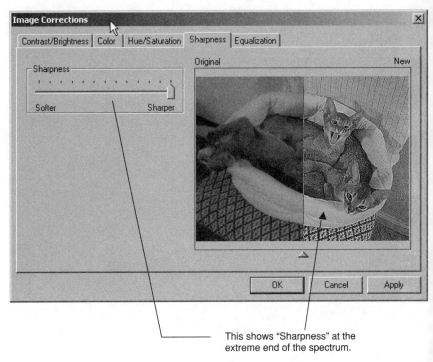

This shows "Sharpness" at the extreme end of the spectrum.

produce a big mess, you have no "Default" button. You will need to cancel everything and start over from the beginning.

The last bit of information about this window is that if you click on "Apply," it is for the full changes in the photograph as you are seeing it. If you click on "OK," it will automatically "Apply" the changes and then close the window. This may not be what you wanted, and the difference between the two buttons may be a bit confusing.

Red Eye

In this program, red-eye removal is not the easiest tool to use. But the advantage of the complicated approach is that it allows for creativity. (This means that if you want someone to have green and purple eyes, you can probably do it.) In order to do a red-eye removal, first zoom in on the area that you want to change. By magnifying the eye it allows you to:

- Do a "One Click Removal," by selecting this option from the menu and clicking on one red pixel on the image. Then you can try clicking on another. If you do not like your correction, click on "Undo" after each "misclick."
- Use a "Brush tool" to sweep over the area and remove the red sections. This is a more advanced technique, because it is easy to erase the "highlight" of the eye while sweeping along. This can be corrected by selecting the "Highlight Brush," which will add a white dot. Again, always be ready to hit the "Undo" button.
- Change the eye color by using the "Correct Any Eye Color" option. If you can manage this well, you can apply for a job in advertising! (See figures 6.8a, 6.8b, 6.9a, and 6.9b.)

Other Fun Tools

The toolbar also includes a "Pen" button and an "Add Text" button. If you select the "Pen" tool, you can draw on the photograph. That means you can add that big red arrow to show your hotel room at the lake, or circle an area that needs closer scrutiny. As always remember that if you do not like the way you made your arrow, you need to click on "Undo" *immediately*. **You can only correct one level back.**

The "Text" button is also a nice addition, as it is a great way of putting descriptions and comments right on the photograph. For both of these tools you can choose different colors. For text you have all the usual writing choices, including different type fonts and sizes.

Figure 6.8a

"Undo" is one of your most important buttons. I think that is why it is first!

The "Red Eye" icon

The easiest way to remove Red Eye is to first try "One Click Removal" or use the "Brush" tool.

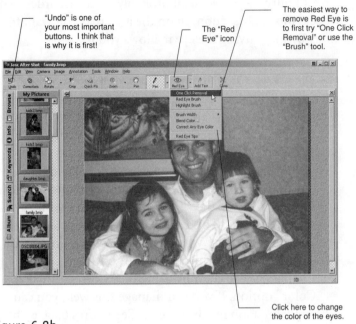

Click here to change the color of the eyes.

Figure 6.8b

Click on the red portion of the eye when using "One Click Removal."

Figure 6.9a

Using the "Red Eye Brush" requires a steady hand, but this lets you cover the red area a bit better.

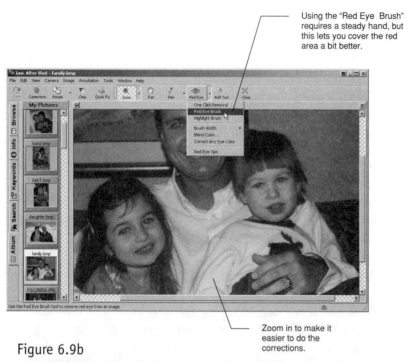

Zoom in to make it easier to do the corrections.

Figure 6.9b

Additional Information

As I mentioned at the beginning of this chapter, there is a new version of After Shot that is called Paint Shop Photo Album. There are a number of very good changes in this program. The first thing you will notice is that the toolbar is rearranged to be more intuitive. The icons on this toolbar are also easier to see and understand. Another major advance is the "Undo" feature that is expanded. You can now go back more than one level if you need to make more than one correction. In addition, the "example" images that come with the program are designed to let you practice the different editing techniques. (The one thing that seems to have been left out is the images you need in order to practice "stitching." However, the description given in chapter 9 should answer most of your questions about this tool.)

One of the more interesting changes is that you now have something called "Adjust Wizard." This is under "Image" on the menu bar. It is a step-by-step guide to editing the "color," "exposure," "vividness," and "sharpness" of an image.

Each of these features is a separate window. In the window you can see the original image and two other possibilities. You then have the option of making changes or keeping your original. This is a quick and easy way not only to see several possibilities, but also to make the changes.

The important options "Quick fix" and "Adjust" are still available. I particularly like "Adjust" as you can fine-tune each change with a slide bar. There is also a new tab called "Flash/Backlighting" that is especially useful. (I cannot tell you the number of times that I forget to consider the bright light behind my main image. The result is a wonderful picture of the background and a dark person in the foreground. This is the tool that will correct this common mistake.) Best of all, the window used to see these changes remains the same as in After

Shot which to my mind is the most accurate way of seeing the "before" and "after" of each image.

The *best* new feature is called "Thinify." That's right. Often you might feel that the image you are seeing must be the camera

"adding" a few pounds. This new tool is the quickest and easiest diet you will ever use to lose those last ten pounds!

Other important features remain similar to the older version. "Keywords" lets you describe and catalogue your images easily. An expanded feature is a tool to send these catalogued images to any backup device you want to use. This also means that your slide shows can be transferred to a CD and viewed on your TV if it has a DVD player. Finally, the additions to the "Audio" editing are impressive. (As with several other programs, you can download a trial version of this program. See Appendix C for more information about this.)

7

Chapter 7
ACDSee™ 5.0

ACDSee, from the company ACD™ Systems™, Ltd., was the first image-editing program that I ever used. Several people suggested to me that it was one of the easiest and best image-editing programs on the market. It has consistently received the "top choice" rating from many important computer magazines, and its advertising claims that it is used by "over 24 million people." There are actually two parts to this program. The first one is primarily for organization, utility, and projects. The second one is an easy image-editing program. Another thing that I really liked about starting with this program is that a free trial period allows you to "test run" the software. The cost of the program itself is between $35 and $45 dollars, depending on promotions.

To start using this program, load the CD onto your computer and answer all the usual questions as it runs through its installation process. (I would really like to know who actually reads the "End User License Agreement." And who would ever consider not accepting it after spending money to buy the program?) One of the questions you will need to answer is whether you want this to be your default image-editing program. Again this is up to you, as you can easily open the program from the "Start" menu. However, in this case you might want to make this the default. It is a good way to see how a program can manage any image that "arrives" on your computer.

You will have the choice of adding several other programs, such as QuickTime. Most of these programs are only necessary to support various multimedia formats. (If you want, you can see the long list of these formats at the beginning of the user manual, but I personally do not understand any of the initials listed. Fortunately there is a list of all the abbreviations in the user manual appendices, if you are really interested. I have been fine without these extra installations.)

One of the downloads you *will* need is FotoCanvas™ Lite. When you go to the "Start" menu and then to "Programs" and

"ACD Systems," you will have a choice of two programs: the main program, ACDSee, and FotoCanvas Lite. Each has its own special uses, which I will discuss below. ACDSee is the organizer and primary program for most tasks. After you are done with all the installations and have restarted your computer, there should be a shortcut for ACDSee on your desktop. If not, you can open the program by clicking on the "Start" menu, selecting "Programs," clicking on "ACD Systems," and then clicking on "ACDSee."

The first window that appears is the full "Browse" window, which is divided into a number of panes. (You can also have a superimposed window that gives you the "Tip of the Day," which I personally like to read. However, you can turn off this feature by deselecting it from the little box on the lower left side of the window. See figure 7.1.)

Figure 7.1

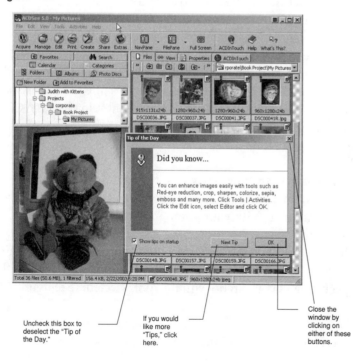

Uncheck this box to deselect the "Tip of the Day."

If you would like more "Tips," click here.

Close the window by clicking on either of these buttons.

The "Browser Bar" is on the left side of the window and has a list of all your folders. In addition it automatically highlights "My Pictures." What this means is that if you have any loose images in this section, they will appear in the primary pane (the "Files" pane) to the right of the Browser Bar. Otherwise find whatever folder you want to use, click on it, and those files will appear as thumbnail images to the right. On the bottom of the window is the Status bar, which gives you all the information about the images in the folder you are viewing and specific information about the individual file you selected. (See figure 7.2.)

Now before moving on, it is important to notice all the added features of the ACDSee Browser Bar. The Browser Bar has a number of tabs on the top of the pane, and you have the ability to create new folders, add folders, and even designate a folder as a "favorite" for easy access. (See figure 7.3.) If you click on "Albums," you have all the current photo albums that are stored in "My Pictures." There is also a tab for "Photo Discs." This is a very special feature that is also very easy to use. If you have stored images on a CD, load the CD into the CD driver of your computer. Click on the "Photo Disc" tab and then click on "New Disc." You can then select specific images or download the whole CD to a folder in this section. Name the folder and you have access to all these images without reloading the CD every time you want to see them. The last tab is "Search" which is self-explanatory.

Going back to the initial window, the bar above the Browser Bar is the "Main Toolbar," and it is filled with all the icons you need to edit and play with your photographs. Most are similar to tools you have used before or are easy to understand. When you click on one of these icons, a new bar appears under the Main Toolbar. This is called the "Activities Toolbar." These are all the specific tasks you can do with the tool selected. (See figure 7.4.)

One of the icons that might be new to you is the "NavPane." This icon (eighth from the left) looks like the Browser window.

Figure 7.2

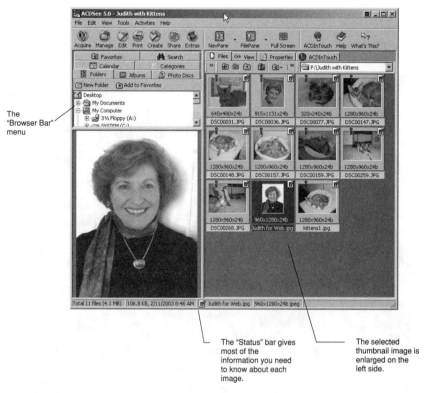

The "Browser Bar" menu

The "Status" bar gives most of the information you need to know about each image.

The selected thumbnail image is enlarged on the left side.

Figure 7.3

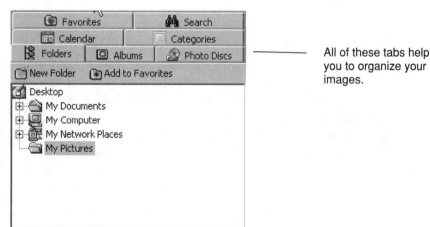

All of these tabs help you to organize your images.

Figure 7.4

Click on the "Edit" icon first
as this will open the editing
program "FotoCanvas Lite."

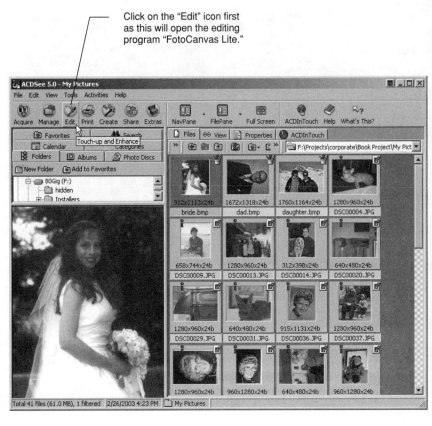

If you click on it, the Browser Bar and "Preview" pane
are eliminated (in other words, all the extra panes). What you
have left is the "FilePane" (your primary pane) with
the thumbnail images you will edit. (See figure 7.5.) Next to the
"NavPane" icon is the "Full Screen" icon. If you click on this icon,
the "FilePane" will fill the entire desktop. In this view, very few
options are available on the simplified toolbar. (See figure 7.6)

Go ahead and click on these different icons and see the number
of tasks you can perform with each tool. An example is the
"Create" tool. If you check the activities bar after clicking on

Figure 7.5

The "Create" icon
shows different
projects.

Click on the "FilePane" button
to eliminate the preview and
browser panes and to see just
the thumbnail images.

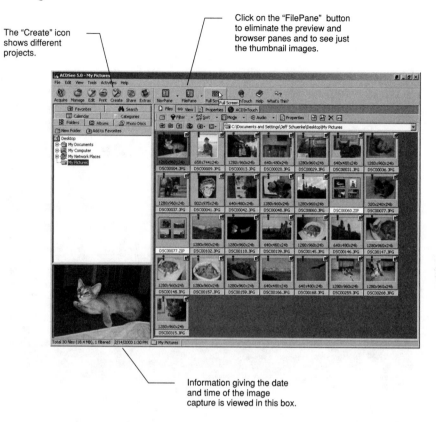

Information giving the date
and time of the image
capture is viewed in this box.

this icon, you have a choice of making an image into wallpaper,
a contact sheet, a combination of photographs in different sizes
for printing, and archiving your images.

The menu bar has all of the same tools and some extra features.
One of the nice features of this program is that many of the
tasks have a "keystroke" equivalent. This means that if you have
trouble using a mouse, you can access most of the commands
using the keyboard. (A list of the commands is in the ACDSee
user manual.) The tool that I want to describe now, however, is
the "Edit" tool.

Figure 7.6

The "FilePane" gives some basic
information about each image.

Click on the "i" or the photo
icon to see everything about
the image.

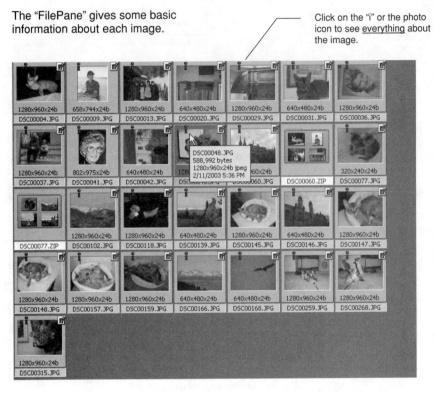

Editing Information

As you look at the thumbnail images in the "FilePane," you
already can see more information about each photo than you
have seen in any of the other image-editing programs. Beneath
each is the "size" of the original photograph, the number of
kilobytes used, the date and time it was taken, its name or
number, and its format. There is also a little letter "i" in green
in the left corner, and a tiny icon of a photograph in the right
corner. If you click on the "i," it is a shortcut to immediately
give you the "Metadata" for this image. This is probably more
information than you know about yourself! It is here that you
can learn everything from the make and model of the camera

Figure 7.7

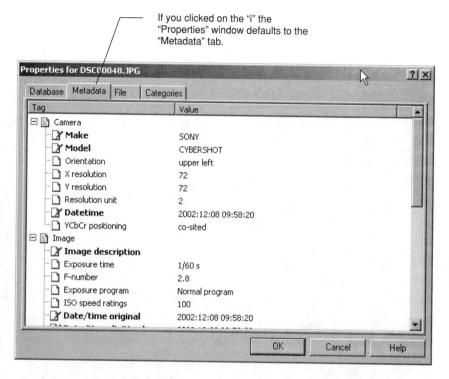

If you clicked on the "i" the "Properties" window defaults to the "Metadata" tab.

that took the photograph to the exposure time, f-number, ISO speed, aperture value, the *precise* time the image was shot and much more. (See figures 7.6 and 7.7.) And you always thought that the only important information in your life was the last four digits of your social security number!

If you click on the image icon on the right side, you get the same "Properties" window, but this time it defaults to the "File" tab. Here things are broken down into "File properties" and "Image attributes." There is a lot of the same information, but it seems to be presented in a friendlier way. (See figure 7.8.)

The last tab is "Database." This tab is very important because this is where you can add pertinent information such as notes and keywords. This means that you will be able to find the photo later

Figure 7.8

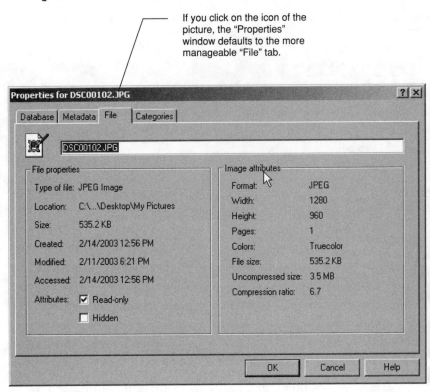

If you click on the icon of the picture, the "Properties" window defaults to the more manageable "File" tab.

on. You can also add the name of the photographer, so there are no arguments later as to who took the fabulous, award-winning photograph of Karen sinking the 30-foot putt. (See figure 7.9.)

You are probably wondering why any of this is important (except perhaps crediting the photograph to yourself). You might recall that in one of the earlier chapters I mentioned that it is important to practice with your camera so that you know how to make adjustments for lighting conditions, speed, focal length, and so on. For many of us, it is difficult to remember these terms, much less understand what they really mean or how they affect our photographs. However, you already understand "garbage in, garbage out," and you want to take the

Figure 7.9

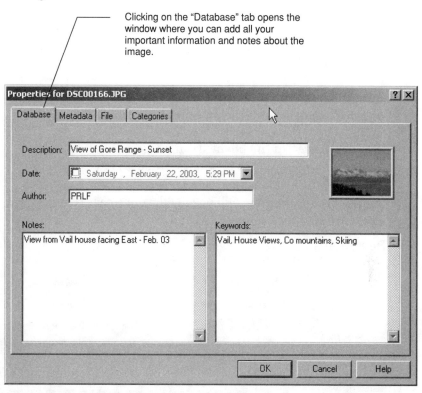

Clicking on the "Database" tab opens the window where you can add all your important information and notes about the image.

best photograph you can. That way there will be less editing to do. Here is the trick: If you can look at an image, notice what is wrong with it, and see the information related to this image, you can then arrange things differently the next time you take a photo. At least I think that is the theory.

Editing an Image

As it turns out, ACDSee is very limited in its editing capabilities. You must first double-click on the image that you want to edit. The "Edit" icon takes you to five different editing tools. Each one of these is simply asking you how you want to handle the basics in editing an image. With "Image Rotate," you can have the adjustments made individually or for all of your photographs. This is more of a "batch" approach to editing. The same is true for "Image Exposure." One of the better tools is "Convert," which allows you to change your image format. If you really want to have a TIFF file instead of the original JPEG, this is the place to make that change.

However, for your real image editing, this is the moment when you want to open the program FotoCanvas Lite.

If you have selected (highlighted) an image in ACDSee that you want to edit, the easy way to open FotoCanvas Lite is to go to "Tools" on the menu bar and select "Open in Editor . . ." (Ctrl + E). The program will open with your image centered in a new window. (See figures 7.10a and 7.10b.)

Figure 7.10a

Click on "Tools on the ACDSee menu bar and then click on "Open in Editor..." form the drop down menu.

The new window is the image editing program "FotoCanvas Lite."

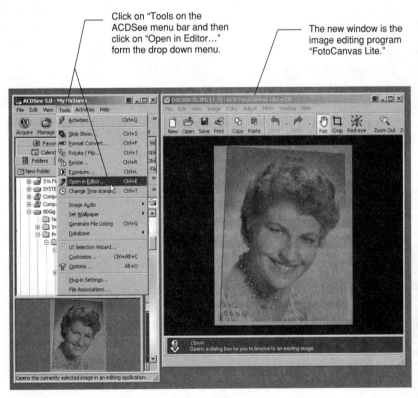

Figure 7.10b

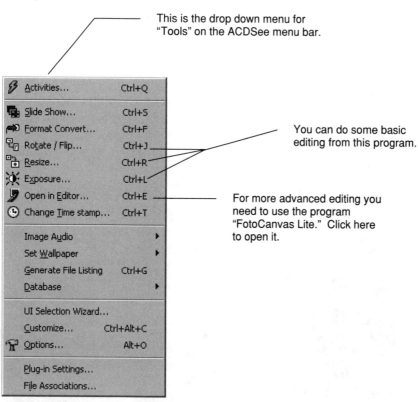

This is the drop down menu for "Tools" on the ACDSee menu bar.

You can do some basic editing from this program.

For more advanced editing you need to use the program "FotoCanvas Lite." Click here to open it.

If you know you just want to edit one particular image, you should go directly to the program. To do this click on the "Start" menu, go to "Programs," highlight "ACD Systems," and click on "FotoCanvas Lite." The next step is to select an image. This can be done by going to the "File" menu and selecting "Open," or clicking on the "Open" icon on the toolbar. Run through the browser to find the folder and then the file with which you want to work. Then click on this file.

One of the advantages of this program is that there are multiple levels of "Undo." (The nuances of this will be discussed later.) As you may have discovered from using or reading about some of the other programs mentioned, a lot of mistakes can be made and extra work is involved when there is only one level of this tool. You must remember to go back to it constantly.

There are many other advantages of FotoCanvas Lite. One is that as you point to a particular icon, there is a helpful information bar at the bottom of the window. In one sentence this information guide explains the function of most of the icons on the toolbar above. This means you have continuous help. (See figure 7.11.) If you check this bar, it also tells you how

Figure 7.11

Both the Menu bar and the Tool bar are easy to use and provide basic editing.

Note the "Help" bar that appears when you point the cursor on an icon.

to progress with each of the tasks once you actually begin to make the changes. I also like the fact that it is easy to stop what you are doing, like a crop, just by going to another part of the image and clicking in an open space. Something else to know is that the menu bar is as easy to use as the toolbar. Finally, you can make corrections in any order that you wish.

Of course there are also disadvantages to this program. It is rather basic, which means there are fewer things with which to play. It does show the before and after images, but the photos are small and difficult to compare. (There is a "Proof" button, so it is possible to see the new image in a larger format before committing to a change.) There is a "Reset" button, but it is not available for every type of adjustment.

Rotate

By this time I am sure you have heard enough about this tool. Rather than have you count fifteen icons from the left to find it, I suggest going from the right side to the left, where it is the fifth icon. This tool works in the same way as the "Rotate" tool in other programs and is intuitive in design.

Crop

The "Crop" tool icon is in the middle of the toolbar. Click on this icon and then point the cursor at a "starting point." Drag the cursor to form a box around the area that you want to select as your image. Now release the left mouse button. There are several dots along the box, and by pointing the cursor on any of them, you can drag the sides of the box in and out to change the original shape. You can also place the cursor in the middle of the box and move the whole box to adjust the exact placement of the crop. However—and this is important—if you double-click inside the crop box, the area outside of the box will be removed. **There is no way to go back to your original image.** Is there any way to have your original and the cropped

image? Yes, if you go to the "File" menu and select "Save as...,"
you can rename the original and/or the cropped image, and
then you will have both.

Resize

To the right of the "Rotate" button is the "Resize" button. When
you click on this tool, you have a choice of adjusting the image
by a percentage of its original size or by pixel dimensions. If you
resize by changing the percentage of the photo, then it might be
best to keep the default setting, "Maintain original aspect
ratio." It is recommended that images be reduced either
33 percent or 50 percent with this setting. If you are changing
the number of pixel to resize, then you can change the width
and the height of the photo while maintaining the aspect ratio.
Or you can uncheck this box to distort the image by making
unusual adjustments. (See figure 7.12.)

The final option given is the "Resampling filter." I had no idea
what this was until I checked the user manual. As you know, when

Figure 7.12

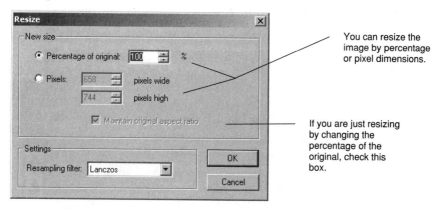

You can resize the image by percentage or pixel dimensions.

If you are just resizing by changing the percentage of the original, check this box.

an image is resized, the pixels are affected. This was discussed in earlier chapters. The seven filters that are offered as part of the "Resize" tool alter the normal changes in the pixels that occur with each resizing. I suggest reading the descriptions of each of these filters and then playing with them a bit to see if you think this is something worth doing. Personally, I think this falls into the category of "the second week with my new digital camera!"

Something else worth noting is the recommendation, in the user manual, to resize an image only once, because resizing changes the position of each pixel in relation to every other pixel. (I never thought about this, but it makes sense.) Of course having read this, I naturally had to repeatedly resize one of my photographs. The manual is absolutely right! If you resize enough, the artifacts and jaggies start popping out, along with some unexpected color distortion.

Red-eye Reduction

As I have used the "Zoom" tool while resizing my photograph, it makes sense to do the red-eye reduction at this time. After zooming in on the eye that needs help, click on the "Red-eye Reduction" button. A "Tool Options" box will appear. Point the cursor on the red area and hold down the left mouse button as you drag the cursor around this area. The shape formed by this process is an ellipse, and if you have selected "Show Outline" from the "Tool Options" box, you can see the shape as it is formed. Then select the amount of the eye color "intensity" that you want. (This is important, because not only are you picking a color for your eye, but this helps to blend the selected color into the natural eye color.) The numbers range from 0 to 255. As eye color is added from the inside out, if you pick the higher number the inside of the eye will be brighter. This is something to consider as you play with the numbers. By the

Figure 7.13

To adjust the intensity and color of the eyes, use the slide on this bar.

The Red-eye reduction icon

First use the "Zoom" tool as it will make it easier to see and work with the eyes.

Note the "Tips" bar that gives you instructions on using this editing tool.

way, when you do pick a color for the eye, you have the usual "driver's license" choices. But you also can choose "Custom . . ." which gives you have a complete palette of colors. You can vary the hue, saturation, and luminescence, too. Think of all the possibilities! (See figures 7.13 and 7.14.)

Auto Levels

As I mentioned originally, when using this program you can follow any order to make most of these corrections. The only thing you need to do to use the Auto Levels correction is to click on the icon. Everything else is done by FotoCanvas Lite.

Figure 7.14

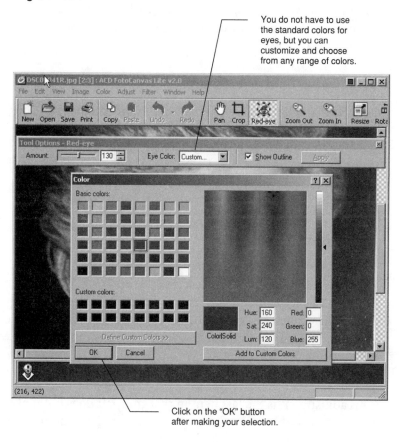

You do not have to use the standard colors for eyes, but you can customize and choose from any range of colors.

Click on the "OK" button after making your selection.

OK, not exactly everything. If you click on the icon, a correction is made—period.

However, if you go to the menu bar and click on "Adjust," there are now two choices. The first is the simple auto correction. The other is an "Exposure . . ." correction. This selection displays a window with several slide controls and the before and after views. If you click on "Auto," you make the same correction that you did before. The big difference is, now you can actually see what the program did to make this correction. The slide buttons move to show the changes in black, white, and gamma correction. You then have the option of further enhancing these changes by sliding the buttons to different settings. The whole thing is not particularly intuitive, but fortunately the next adjustment is brightness, contrast, and gamma (again). (See figure 7.15.)

Brightness/Contrast/Gamma

For this correction you see the same window whether you click on the icon or go to the menu bar. This is the moment when you might want to review the differences among these three adjustments as described in Chapter 4. The diagrams there will also help explain what happens when you make changes in these light values.

Hue/Saturation/Lightness

The only way to make these changes is to go to the menu bar, click on "Adjust," and then select Hue/Saturation/Lightness. The window for this adjustment also has slide controls. The suggested sequence is logical, because when you change the hue and saturation, the brightness will also need an adjustment.

Red/Green/Blue

This adjustment is the last item in this group. It does not make sense to me, but I did not create this program. I also do not like

114

Figure 7.15

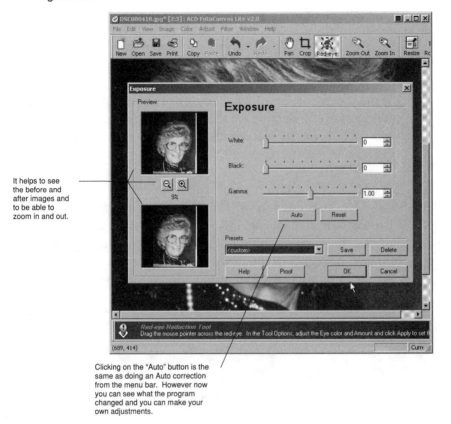

It helps to see the before and after images and to be able to zoom in and out.

Clicking on the "Auto" button is the same as doing an Auto correction from the menu bar. However now you can see what the program changed and you can make your own adjustments.

the fact that the only colors listed are red, green, and blue. This assumes that everyone knows and understands the opposite colors and knows how to make these corrections without a lot of experimenting. For use in a basic editing program, I think this is a tremendous disadvantage.

Additional Information

This program lets you have some fun playing with different filters to produce negative or sepia images. There are also techniques to blur, sharpen, emboss, paint, draw, and more.

115

Best of all, when everything is a real mess, there is a way to rescue your original image. Click on the "File" menu and select "Revert." Now you have your original photograph without all the silly filters, colors, or purple eyes. **Important:** *The "Revert" command cannot change a mistake in cropping.* Review that section to ensure that you do not mess up your image. Also, it is my mistake to say, "Now you have your *original* photograph . . . ." Because we all know that you should *never* work on the original—only make changes to a copy of the original.

My one other suggestion is this, and it applies to all the computer programs you will ever use. **Learn how to use the "Escape/Cancel" (Esc) key**. Hitting this key is the same as pointing the cursor on the "Cancel" button and clicking once. You have no idea how often you will want to cancel whatever you are doing while working with an image-editing program. I practically lived with my finger on the "Esc" key while writing this book.

Chapter 8
Adobe® Photoshop®
Elements 2.0

Photoshop Elements 2.0 by Adobe® Systems, Inc., is the most advanced program I will discuss in this book. It is also the most expensive, as it costs anywhere from $75 to $100. Adobe is a company that has traditionally made the software used by professionals for commercial design purposes. Therefore it has many features that the ordinary person would not need, especially when starting basic digital image editing. For this reason the company has made the program Photoshop Elements, which is user-friendly and a simpler version of their commercial software.

The reality is that about 90 percent of the commercial tools are included in Photoshop Elements, so the software is not really limited at all. But it is neither a problem nor too confusing to have these "little extras," even though you will probably only use a few of them. Photoshop Elements is a full-feature photo-manipulation program, and as such it gives you "room to grow." In fact as your skills progress, you might want to play with some of the features for which Adobe software is famous, such as drawing and painting, dodging and burning, stitching, cloning, and so on.

118

Installation

The first thing to do is to install the program by putting the CD into the CD drive of you computer and then watching as the set-up begins. You are offered a choice of languages, which is a nice touch, and then asked whether you want to "install or explore"—go for install. Photoshop Elements and Photoshop Acrobat are your next choices, and of course you want Elements. Then you are asked one more time about your language selection. If you made the wrong selection the first time around, this gives you a second chance—assuming you have understood the last few directions in Swahili. Keep clicking "Next," filling in all the information required and saving everything to the default destination. Now if you want, you can go to the "Read Me" file, but I would uncheck this box and click on "Finish." Once you restart your computer you will find the Photoshop Elements icon as a shortcut on your desktop.

When you open Photoshop Elements for the first time, you will see a "Welcome" window that offers all sorts of information, including a tutorial. This tutorial is similar to normal help files and is static. My suggestion is that this book and/or the user guide will be much more helpful. Just turn off this screen for now. You can always return to it by going to the "Help" menu. In addition, there is a "Quick Reference Card" that comes with the user guide.

The Primary Window

The most important thing to do, as with all these programs, is to familiarize yourself with the "work area." This window looks a little more complicated than the ones you have seen in the previous programs. Just take some time to look at each area separately and it will not be so overwhelming. On the top is the traditional menu bar. Below that is what they call the "shortcuts bar," with the icons you are used to using and a few extra features. (See figures 8.1a and 8.1b.)

Figure 8.1a

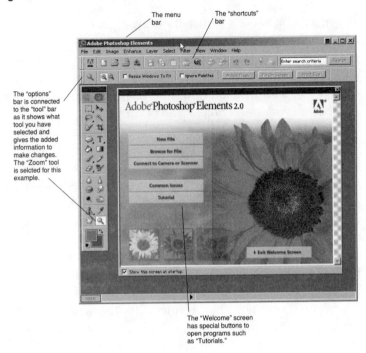

The menu bar

The "shortcuts" bar

The "options" bar is connected to the "tool" bar as it shows what tool you have selected and gives the added information to make changes. The "Zoom" tool is selcted for this example.

The "Welcome" screen has special buttons to open programs such as "Tutorials."

Figure 8.1b

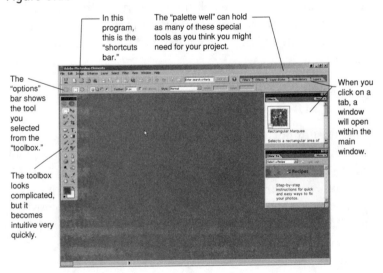

In this program, this is the "shortcuts bar."

The "palette well" can hold as many of these special tools as you think you might need for your project.

The "options" bar shows the tool you selected from the "toolbox."

The toolbox looks complicated, but it becomes intuitive very quickly.

When you click on a tab, a window will open within the main window.

Below that is an "options bar." This is actually connected to the "toolbox," which is the vertical box on the left side of the window. When you select a tool, the options bar lists the default settings for that tool and then allows you to change these settings to meet your needs. For example, if you are drawing a line, you might want to change the width of the line and its color. An even better example is how you can use the "Zoom" tool. (The magnifying glass on the bottom right side of the toolbox.) Click on this icon and notice the changes on the options bar. On the left is the icon you selected—a way of checking that you are working with the tool you wanted to use. With the buttons to the right, you can click on the positive or negative magnifying glass for zooming in or out. Then you can resize windows to fit the screen, find out what the image will look like when printed, and also check ratios that are predefined, such as pixels which are a 1:1 ratio. (See figure 8.2.) Almost all of these icons and boxes have balloons or "tool tips" that explain what each one is or does. Rest your cursor on each of them for a minute to see these labels.

The main center area is the "active image area," the place where you will see your photograph. When you are working with different tools, it is in this window that you will see all the adjustment controls and the "before" and "after" thumbnail images.

Palettes

The special feature that will seem most unfamiliar to you is on the right side of the work area. This area is the "palette well" and it contains "palettes." What are a palette well and palettes? The palette well is a section that holds a number of devices that are useful for image editing and keeping track of your images and their modifications. These devices are called palettes. If you click on "Window" from the menu bar, you can see the variety of palettes that are available. (See figures 8.3 and 8.4.)

121

Figure 8.2

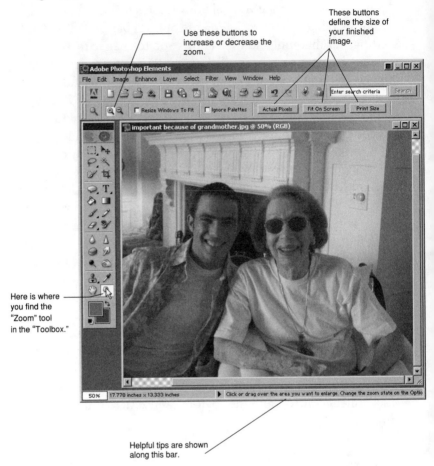

If you click on one of these palettes, it will appear on the work area. You can keep it there and work with it as you please, or click and drag it to the palette well. (A new tab appears to show that it is in the "well.") This saves time, as you have these different schemes at your fingertips rather than going to the "Window" drop-down menu all the time. The palettes can either sit open on the work area or be hidden. You can also see helpful tips about each one of them from the "Hints" pallets and "Recipe." In addition there is a visual, which is the best way

122

Figure 8.3

To choose different palettes, click on "Window" on the menu bar.

If you want extra tips or information on how to do different tasks, add these palettes to the "palette well" or keep them on the open window.

The "palette well"

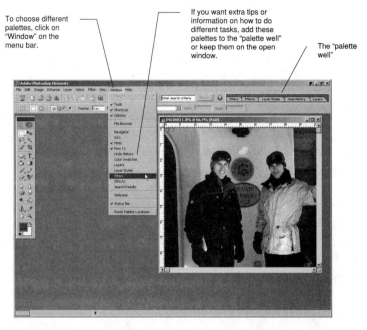

Figure 8.4

These palettes can be moved around or hidden in the "palette well."

The "palette well"

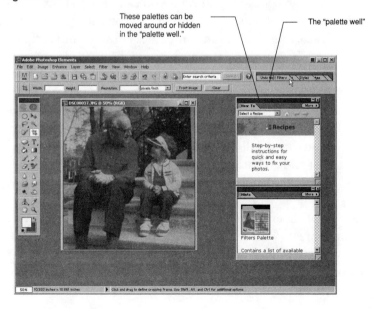

to learn about all the different effects, colors, filters, and such that you can use.

Best of all, there are two features that you will find indispensable: the "How To" palette and the "Undo History" palette. When you click on the "How To" tab, a box drops down. This tells you, step-by-step, how to do all of the editing techniques for the tool selected. It does this by presenting each one of these editing tools as a "Recipe." (See figure 8.5.) When you need help, this palette guides you through the task and even offers to do some of the steps for you. (Now that you know about this feature, I suppose you do not have to read the rest of this chapter, because this palette tells you almost everything that I can.) The "Undo History" tab provides a drop-down menu that shows you all the steps that you have already done in editing your image. It also acts like a "Help" icon and it performs tasks like a shortcut menu. (See figure 8.6.)

The "Undo History" palette is important for two reasons:

- With most other programs you can only go back (undo) one step if you do not like the correction you have made. Also, one change can sometimes affect the other changes you have made. After a while, you have no idea what steps you have done to produce the image in front of you.
- "Undo History" shows each of the steps of your image editing. Every change to the original image is tracked. If you can see all the steps, you can pick one of them on the list and go back to that level. In fact you can go all the way back to the original image and start over again.

As a practical example, you might think of an image that you want to create with several separate elements. Let's start with a photograph of mountains. Perhaps the lighting, color, or cropping needs to be changed on this photo. After making those changes, you want to include the nice picture of the kids

Figure 8.5

The "How To" palette is considered to be like a recipe book.

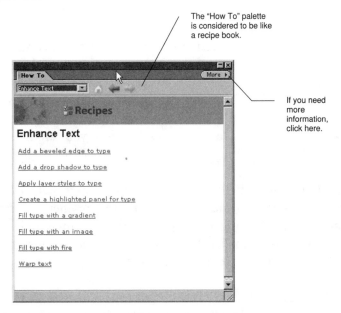

If you need more information, click here.

Figure 8.6

The "Undo History" palette has the great advantage of taking you back as many steps as necessary to rework the image.

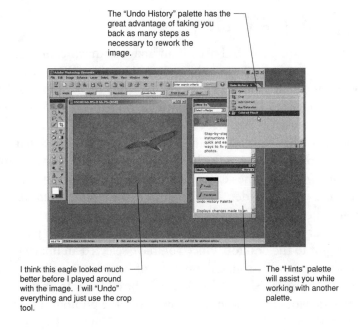

I think this eagle looked much better before I played around with the image. I will "Undo" everything and just use the crop tool.

The "Hints" palette will assist you while working with another palette.

that you took the day before. This photograph can be "laid over" the first image as a separate layer. It is on top of the first. Finally you want to add a big snowperson off to the side. However, this image needs resizing and a color adjustment so it does not look darker than the other photos. Each of these images requires a number of changes. As they were all separate layers, the different changes, like the color and resizing, were done without affecting the other images. The "Undo History" palette can take you to any of these layers so you can make other changes without compromising the original elements.

The last thing to mention about the work area is that all of these extra palettes and bars can be moved to other places by clicking and dragging. Other programs allow you to hide a pane or make it smaller. This one lets you place it where you will find it both convenient and easy to use.

So having said all this, it is time to select an image and see how to do our usual edits using the program Photoshop Elements.

Opening a Folder

The first thing you will need is an image with which to work. To open an image you can either select "Open" or "Browse..." from the "File" menu or click on the icons on the shortcut bar. Let's do it each way. First go to the menu bar and click on "File." When you select "Browse...," the "File Browser" window will pop up. This looks like many of the browser windows that you have already used. On the left you have a list of everything on your computer. The center has the folders and files in the primary image folder, "My Pictures." If you have saved some photographs to your desktop, you can either scroll through the browser or click on the down arrow of the top box to go straight to the desktop. Once you have selected an image from a folder, you will see an enlargement of the photo in the middle pane on the left side. Below that will be all the information anyone would ever want to know about the photograph.

126

At the very bottom of the views of the images, there is a very small bar that lets you change aspects of the "file name," change the size of the images, and do a simple rotation. If you want to play with your selected photograph a bit or see all of them at one time, click on the "More" button at the top right corner of the window. This is the "file browser" menu, and it gives you more options for organizing, renaming, and moving your files. If you pick "Select All" and then click on "Open," you can compare all of the images. This might help you decide which to delete and which are worth editing. (See figure 8.7.)

The other way to do this, which I actually prefer, is to click on the "Open" icon, which is the third one from the left. It gives

Figure 8.7

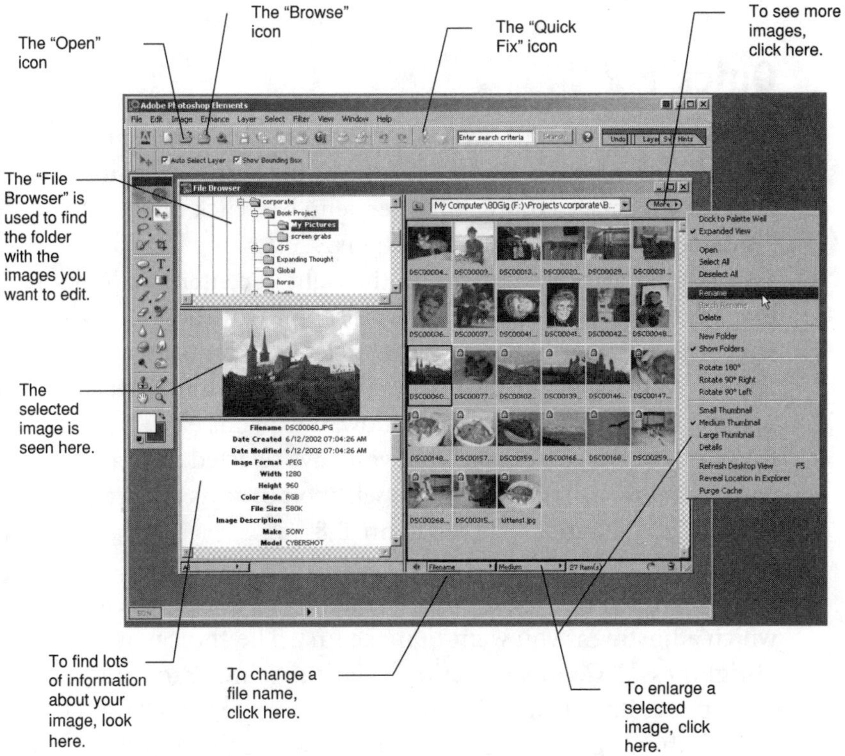

The "Browse" icon

The "Quick Fix" icon

To see more images, click here.

The "Open" icon

The "File Browser" is used to find the folder with the images you want to edit.

The selected image is seen here.

To find lots of information about your image, look here.

To change a file name, click here.

To enlarge a selected image, click here.

127

me the option of picking a new folder or automatically opening the folder on which I was working. Select an image, and with a few clicks you can now see your photograph in a size that is easy to edit. (Of course you can also open "Browse" by clicking on the icon; it is just to the right of the "Open" icon.) Do whatever you prefer so that you will have a photograph in front of you.

Note: It is time to start editing. However in this chapter, I will reverse the order of things slightly. Normally the first thing to do is to rotate the image and then crop it. That way you are working with something that you can easily see, and you're working on the actual part of the photograph that you want as your final image. Photoshop Elements has a special tool for doing most of your editing. Therefore, I think the best place to start in this program is with "Quick Fix." Read on and you will see what I mean.

Quick Fix

As always, there are two ways to open each of the tools, and "Quick Fix" is no exception. It is one of the best tools you will ever use for image editing. On the menu bar, click on "Enhance" and then select "Quick Fix...." On the icon or shortcut bar, click on the icon to the right of center that looks like a diamond with a lightning bolt shooting through it. When you click on either of these, the "Quick Fix" window will appear. At the top are reasonably sized "Before" and "After" images. Below that is a "Tip" window. It explains exactly how to make any of the corrections that you have selected from the choices below it. The steps in the selection process are even labeled "1," "2," and "3"! (See figure 8.8.)

After you open the "Quick Fix" window, you need to decide which adjustment you want to make first. The choices are "Brightness," "Color Correction," "Focus" (similar to "Sharpness/Blur"), and "Rotate." As the first step, click on the radio button for "Brightness." Step 2 asks you to select the

Figure 8.8

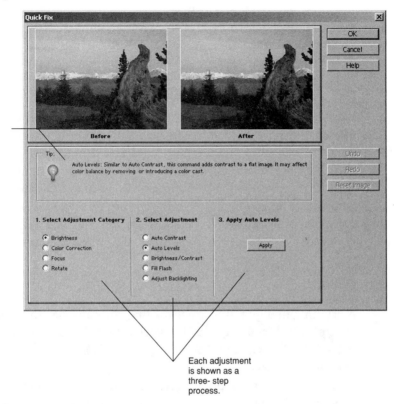

Helpful tips are easy to find.

Each adjustment is shown as a three- step process.

actual adjustment for "Brightness." The choices here are "Auto Contrast," "Auto Levels," "Brightness/Contrast," "Fill Flash," and "Adjust Backlighting." (These last two choices are very nice features, as these are things we all tend to mess up.) In this example, the first two choices, "Auto Contrast" and "Auto Levels," only give you the option "Apply." However the next items have a "Step 3," and it offers several adjustments. **Even better, the "Tip" box explains exactly what these adjustments are and how to do them.**

What I find interesting is that if you select "Brightness" and then "Auto Contrast," the program suggests that you first do a color correction. What this means to me is that the first items in the "Adjustment category" are positioned in the order that is the most logical way to normally do edits. It is interesting that the program suggests doing a color correction first, because changes to contrast and auto levels affect all of these changes. (In other words, if you do not change the color first you will be redoing corrections forever.) Another point worth mentioning is that you can "Undo" as many levels back as you need. You can even completely undo every change by clicking on the "Reset" button. Finally, you can always move the "Quick Fix" window over to the side so that you can see a larger image showing all the changes you have made. This is important, because if you correct the "Contrast" or "Focus" and sharpen your image, it may look fine in the smaller format. Once you view it in its printable version, however, you might not like seeing all the jaggies (not to mention the enhanced wrinkles, pores, and pimples).

What should now be obvious is that this one window can do everything in digital image editing that you can do with all the controls of all the programs discussed in the earlier chapters. As this is *The First Week with My New Digital Camera,* it would be enough to discuss the "Crop" tool and leave it at that. Also you should know that you do not even have to use the "Quick Fix" window. If you want to have instant access to any of these tools, click on "Enhance" or "Image" on the menu bar or click on the appropriate icons. You can always use any of the tools individually. *The biggest advantage of the "Quick Fix" window, as opposed to the individual tools, is that this is the only window in which you can see the before and after images.*

Color Variations

Obviously, there are still many other things you can do with your photograph using this program. One of the tools that I think is a great learning tool, and wonderful to play with, is "Color Variations." The icon for this tool is to the right of "Quick Fix" and looks like three intertwined circles. If you click on this icon, the new window shows the before and after views of your image. Then there is the "Tip" section. Below this is the area in which to experiment. It is also the place where you can really see what it means to increase or decrease colors, brightness, and saturation. In this area you can see your image reproduced eight ways, and each one of these thumbnail photos will teach you something. Of course there is a real reason for having this tool, and it is not for fun and games! However, I am not going to bother with all the technicalities right now and will just use it as a learning tool. You are welcome to check out the various aspects of this tool in the user guide. (See figure 8.9.)

Figure 8.9

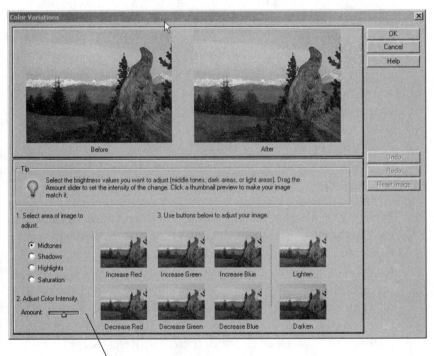

Color variations can be difficult to understand so this window is available for you to experiment and see the image "After" you try different buttons.

Step 1 asks you to select something in the image to change. There are four choices: "Midtones," "Shadows," "Highlights," and "Saturation." Click on each of these radio buttons and see how the sample images change—and this is without actually making any adjustments within that selection. Now pick "Highlights." First click on one of the images and watch the increasing and/or decreasing color changes. Then adjust the color intensity and see the additional changes in the samples.

This is one of the best ways to see that there is an actual difference between "Increase Red" and "Decrease Green." In the traditional way of thinking, red is the complementary color of green. Everyone's natural reaction is to think that if they want to alter their image a bit, they can get the same results by just increasing one *or* decreasing the other. But if you remember the color wheel, then the differences in the images make sense. The fact is that the real opposite of red is cyan and the opposite of green is magenta. There are still other ways of making all these adjustments, but they get really complicated. For example, the color yellow can be changed by either using the two adjacent colors or its opposite color. In other words, yellow is decreased by adding blue or by decreasing red and green. This might seem to be more than any of us needs to know, but again it is part of an equation.

Now go ahead and adjust the amount of intensity you want for the "Highlights." Then click on one of the images. You will see it above as "After." Try clicking on the "Brightness" image that you like. (As you may recall, you often have to make brightness corrections with color changes.) Have fun and keep clicking on different colors to keep adding changes, or hit "Undo" each time and just make one change at a time. The nice thing about all this is that, when all else fails, there is a "Reset Image" button. This means you can play some more, or end the session knowing you have not made a mess of everything.

Once again I must apologize. In my excitement over all the wonderful things that you can do with 'Quick Fix" and the things you can learn about color with the "Color Variations" window, I have not followed the step-by-step format used to describe editing as it is done in all the other programs. I will devote the rest of this chapter to the editing tools that still need to be described.

Rotate

Just in case you were looking for this heading, it is included here for the sake of symmetry. This is normally the first thing to do with a photograph. But it is one of the options in Adobe Photoshop's "Quick Fix," so that is the reason I did not mention it earlier. However, you can also do a rotation by going to "Image" on the menu bar and selecting "Rotate." There are fourteen choices for rotations, from the normal 90 degrees left and right to straightening an image, to working with one layer on top of another. The one thing that I find interesting is that there is a rotation to correct for a crop that is skewed. What this tells me is that the people who wrote this software think it is better to crop before rotating. (Check the user guide, which has the same organization.)

Crop

There are two ways to access the "Crop" tool. One way is to click on "Image" on the menu bar and select "Crop." However if you do this, you get an error message that tells you to select some "pixels." This means that you must first go to the toolbox and choose the "Lasso" tool, the "Rectangular Marquee" tool, or another tool; pick a starting point on your image; draw around the area you want to use; make slight adjustments; right-click for more options; and/or go to "Image" on the menu bar and then select "Crop." If you are not sure about what you are doing at any point, just click on any area outside of the image to clear the blinking lines around the image.

(In addition, the "Undo" option is always there to help you out if you do not like what you have done.)

The other way to access the "Crop" tool is to use the "Crop" icon, which looks like a rectangular box with drawn outlines. You will not find it on the toolbar; it is not there. It is in the "toolbox" (top section, third down on the right). Click on the "crop" icon, and it appears on the options bar along with boxes to show the new dimensions of your cropped image. (See figures 8.10a and 8.10b.) To do a crop, place the cursor on the upper left side of the area you want to enclose. Hold down the left mouse button and drag the cursor to the other side of the image. The exact dimensions and the exact placement of this box are really not that important. Notice that there are little boxes in the corners and on the sides of the selected area. If you place the cursor on one of these boxes and hold down the left mouse button, you can drag or push the line to create a new

Figure 8.10a

The "Crop" icon

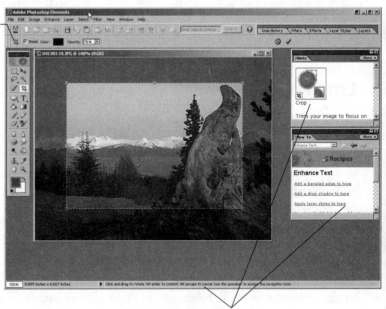

Helpful tips are everywhere.

Figure 8.10b

To change
dimensions, click
and drag any of the
eight boxes around
the crop line.

DSC00139.JPG @ 100% (RGB)

The cropped area
appears lighter.

dimension. Also, the little circle in the center of the box lets you
move the whole selected area around the entire image. As with
the other programs, the area of the new image is lighter than
the area that will be eliminated. **Look at the bottom of the
window. All the information about the size of the crop plus a
set of helpful tips is sitting there**. (See figure 8.10a.) Once
again, if all else fails, click on the "Crop" icon and you have a
choice of "Crop," "Cancel," or "Don't Crop." There is also my

favorite, the "Esc" key. (Yes, I know there are other things that you can see on the options bar, and it means you can play with the photograph in different ways, but quite frankly they are not part of *The First Week*.)

Red Eye

The way to eliminate red eye with Photoshop Elements is by using something called the "Red Eye Brush." This is in the toolbox, second section, fourth icon on the right. It looks like a red eye with a brush. On the options bar you can choose the size of the brush and whether it has hard or soft edges. You can also pick its size (in pixels). Let the cursor sit on any of the "brush strokes" and you will understand the different choices. The "Size" adjustment is the size of the tool, and this really depends on how far you want to zoom in. (See figure 8.11.)

Color selections are the next boxes to the right—they show the current color and the replacement color. If you have "First Click" as the default ("Sampling" on the right), the current color refers to the spot where you first placed the cursor on the image and clicked. The alternative is to pick one of the colors on your photo. The new color will appear on the bottom of the toolbox. Finally, you can click on "Replacement" and choose a color from a complete palette of colors. (See figure 8.12.)

This window shows the current color choice on the box to the right, but in the main pane there is a graduated chart of color selections. You can pick one of these by clicking on it. There are slight variations that are shown at the bottom of your selection box. The key here is to check the colors in the "Current" and "Replacement" boxes on the options bar or at the bottom of the toolbox. The first place you click will take the old color and replace it with the new color. (This process can also be tricky. However, the palette offers many choices, and if you want more options you can go to "Window" on the menu bar and click on "Color Swatches.")

Figure 8.11

The first step is to click on the "Red Eye Brush" icon.

Figure 8.12

Click on the down arrow for more options.

The current color

The replacement color

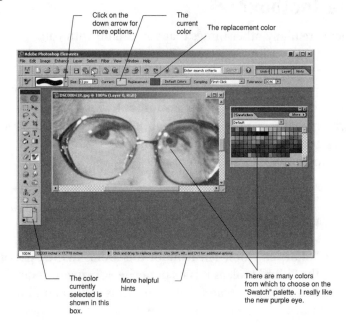

The color currently selected is shown in this box.

More helpful hints

There are many colors from which to choose on the "Swatch" palette. I really like the new purple eye.

137

The last choice on the options bar is "Tolerance." If you set this very low, the pixel color you choose will only change the pixel colors around the original pixel. Also it will change it with something that is close to the original color. This is very limiting. It is best to average a default of 30 percent. Why only 30 percent? If you go to a higher default, then all the colors will fit the parameters and this will not help you very much.

Important: Correcting for red eye is very difficult and takes practice. Please use the "Help" tips and try to go through the sections in the user guide about this correction. One of the most important hints to make the job easier is to enlarge the area within which you want to work. Use the "Zoom" tool to make the eye as large as you can, so that you can really see the areas that needs changes.

Extras: What are All the Other Icons in the Toolbox?

There are many other things that you can do with your photographs using Photoshop Elements. Below are some of the more basic tools to take you to the next level. They can all be found in the toolbox. (Check the Quick Reference Card for the locations and the user guide for more specifics as to how to use each one of them.) I strongly recommend that you find a bad photograph of a person and play with that in order to experiment with these different tools.

- **"Blur" tool:** By clicking and dragging this tool in a particular area, you can do things like taking out wrinkles.
- **"Sharpen" tool:** The icon for this tool is to the right of the "Blur" tool, as it is its opposite. It brings out detail. You need to be careful with this. It is easy to do too much, and then you are left with artifacts. The best

138

technique here is to enlarge the area of the image by zooming in and then working a little bit at a time.

- **"Sponge" tool:** One uses the sponge to blend colors. Blending colors gives the image a softer, subtler look. It is like using a wet sponge when painting with watercolors.

- **"Smudge" tool:** This tool can either rub colors together in an area, or it can take a new color and wipe it all over the image. This is the tool to use for painting on a mustache or dragging lipstick all over a face.

- **"Dodge" and "Burn" tools:** These tools are used to lighten and darken specific areas of a photograph. These are among the tools that correct for exposure mistakes. The "Dodge" tool has the effect of decreasing exposure, which lightens an area, and the "Burn" tool does the opposite. Again these are tools to play with, *carefully*. Work with a small area. Pick the size and style of brush, but keep in mind that there is a big difference between using a fuzzy one or a sharp one. With the "Dodge" tool, start out by single-clicking across a person's forehead to lighten an area that might be in shadows. See how you like the changes. With the "Burn" tool, you are darkening an area, so try fixing a shiny nose or an area that caught the flash incorrectly. You might even try working on the reflection of a jewelry chain that is distracting.

Obviously there are many more things you can do with your photographs with this program. After all, this is primarily known as a painting and drawing program. I think that the tools mentioned above are fun and at the same time reasonably easy to use and master. The whole thing comes down to how much you want to do with the files and folders of photographs that are sitting on your desktop. I think that most of the time, simple corrections are sufficient.

However, if you have a very special photograph that needs some enhancement to make it the perfect gift, this is the program that can do it. Remember to first practice on something unimportant. Then make a copy (or several) of your special image so that you will always have the original in case something goes wrong in the editing process.

Organization

Having talked a lot about editing images with Photoshop Elements, I've said very little about how to organize them. In many ways you handle your photographs here as you do in all the other programs. Download the images to a specific folder in "My Pictures" or to a folder on the desktop. Next name each of the images. This, however, is normally not the thing any of us wants to do. Therefore we have a pile of folders with nameless files. (Numbers do not help—ever!) Luckily, this program offers a method of converting several photographs to new formats, different sizes and resolutions, new names with subcategories, and so on, by using something called the "Batch" command. This is a very useful tool. Click on "File" on the menu bar to find it. It puts everything you need together in one window. However, it is a bit complicated to describe each of the options, so if this is something that interests you, please refer to the user guide.

Helpful Hints

Here are just a few extra thoughts that I probably should have mentioned at the beginning of this chapter. I would have done this except these things are complicated changes and most people will not need them. Also, it would only have delayed getting to the important aspects of editing.

You already know that the monitor and the printer show and produce colors differently. The image you view on the screen will not look exactly the same when printed. One of the ways to work with this is to recalibrate the monitor. In this way you know that whatever you see on one monitor will carry over to other monitors, the Web, and other printers. All of this involves adjusting a whole group of settings. Fortunately all of this is explained in the user guide. When you are actually trying to follow these instructions, remember to click on the "Wizard" button, which will explain each change step by step. The idea is that it is best to start at a known level which means that your monitor profile is the same as other monitors. It is a way of having accurate color management. The monitor is trying to make a match that is as close as it can be to what the program "thinks" it is showing you. If you do not like what you see after making the usual corrections, you might consider trying this recalibration. It is internationally recognized and known as ICC profiles. (ICC stands for International Color Consortium.)

One more feature to mention here has to do with how you are going to use your images. If you know you are going to use your images on the Web, look for the tool that limits the colors you can use to those that are Web compatible. (This can be changed by clicking on "Start," "Control Panel," and "Display;" then change the color setting to 256 colors.) In that way your images will show up looking the same on every browser.

9

Chapter 9

Great—You Have Your Edited Images and They are Named and Organized. Now What? It's Time to Look at Projects.

The title of this chapter implies that after all your hard work, there is still more to do. However, as Gershwin said in the opera *Porgy and Bess,* "It Ain't Necessarily So." You have taken a photograph, you have named the photograph and the folder within which it sits, you have made the photograph look great with editing, and you have saved this image to the hard drive of your computer. (At least I hope you have saved it!) You may have even gone so far as to save your folders to several CDs so you can send all the photographs of your trips, or Ali and Jason's birthday party, to your family and friends.

So this is the question: are you done? Well, that is up to you. If you think about it, you can stop at this stage because this is probably more than you ever did with the photographs taken with your old 35-millimeter camera. These other images are probably sitting in boxes in the basement, mixed together with lots of unrecognizable negatives. Or maybe you do have them organized in nice albums, but they are still in the basement and are taking up three shelves of a bookcase. (Now if you are really having fun with your editing program, I should point out that one of the things you can do with your new skills, and some extra hardware, is to scan all those old photographs into your computer, edit them, and organize them into beautiful albums. OK, relax, this is just a joke. I understand that this was not the first thing you had in mind—it was just a suggestion.) However, getting back to the original question, there are many fun and interesting projects you can do with your edited images. It is really just a matter of time, enthusiasm, and imagination.

One of the great things about digital photography is that you have your own images and they are inside your computer. This means you can use your computer to create a variety of art projects, gifts, special effects, and more. Each of the programs covered in the previous chapters will do many of the following tasks:

- Printing the images in multiple ways, from a contact sheet to a variety of sizes.

- Adding text messages and comments directly on the photograph.
- Sending e-mail to family and friends.
- Organizing the images into albums that can be uploaded to the Web. (Then they can be seen by others easily and even printed out by them directly.)
- Creating your own Web pages.
- Inserting images into other applications, such as a text document.
- Stitching together a series of images.
- Changing the appearance of images to make them look like paintings, drawings, old-fashioned photographs, etc.
- Putting together your own greeting cards, announcements, calendars, and invitations.
- Using your photographs instead of the usual pre-loaded images as computer screen-savers, wallpaper, slide shows, etc.

However, each program has a different approach to these things. I think some of the programs make it much easier to do

creative projects such as announcements and invitations than others. Some programs are geared more towards Web pages and online photo albums. In any case, I think it is something you need to think about when weighing the advantages and disadvantages of using a particular program. Of course I have one other solution to the problem of liking one program for its editing capabilities and another for its easy and clever approach to projects. This is something I will discuss at the end of the chapter. At this point, let's just look at the four different programs and check out a variety of projects that they enable you to do.

Microsoft Picture It!

Picture It! is a program that emphasizes all the fun things you can do with your photographs. The "Companion Guide" devotes the last five chapters (out of 12) to showing you how to do a number of projects. On the original start-up window, it has an icon that directs you to a list of these creative projects along with a "Help Center" that is easy to access and understand. If you do not want to see the start-up window each time you open the program, you will first see the work area window. This window has easy visual access for creating projects, as the "Common Tasks" bar is to the left and you have lots of space to "Create a project..." when you click on this task.

There is a trick to starting a project. You should first select a photograph (or several photographs) with which to work. Then you should be ready to insert the Picture It! disk into the CD drive, as it holds all the templates and special effects you will want to access. (This is one good reason not to lend your disks to your friends.) The images you have selected will be sitting in the tray at the bottom of the work area. The easy way to start a project is to go to the "Common Tasks" list and click on the icon that is the second from the bottom, "Create a project...." You can also find this on the menu bar under "File." (See figures 9.1a and 9.1b)

146

Figure 9.1a

To create a project either click on the icon or go to "File" on the menu bar and select it from there.

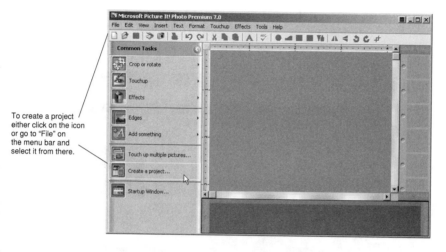

Figure 9.1b

If you select "Create a project…," these are the twelve projects that are available in this program.

Pick one of the twelve different projects by clicking one of the titles.

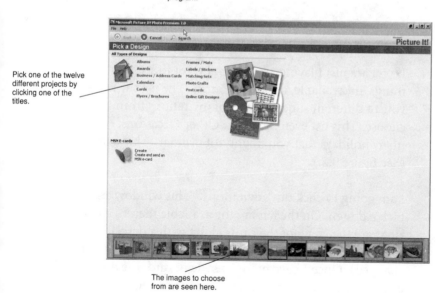

The images to choose from are seen here.

147

Figure 9.2

You can see the different themes to choose from in this box.

You will need to have the Picture It! CD available and in place in the CD drive to see these templates.

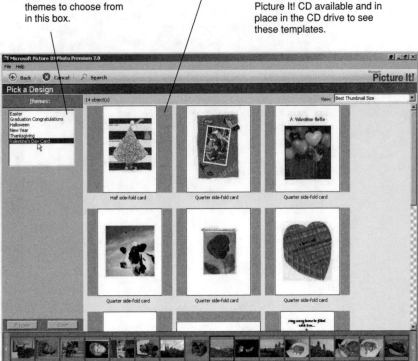

If you are just playing around and want to see what kind of things are available, click on "Cards." The next window gives you 14 different subcategories of invitations from which to choose. This list even includes "Other Occasions," which covers many holidays that you might not ordinarily have on your list. (See figure 9.2.)

I am going to click on "Invitations." This window asks me to pick a design. On the left are the available themes and on the right are the views of the cards along with a description of how they open and the different folding styles (which can be changed). Once I have picked a style of card, the different views of this are shown on the lower left of the window. To work on

Figure 9.3

The text, the image, and the template are separate layers. Each are placed one on top of the other to produce the finished design.

Editing tools are still available.

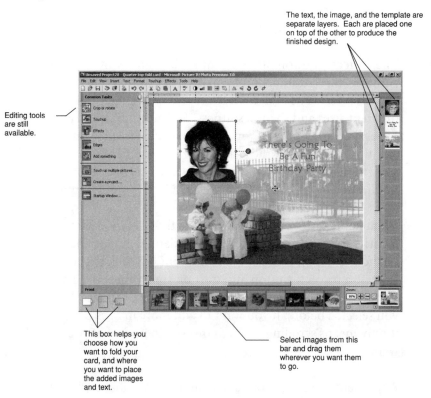

This box helps you choose how you want to fold your card, and where you want to place the added images and text.

Select images from this bar and drag them wherever you want them to go.

the front, middle, or back of the card, I click on the correct icon. If I have picked out several photographs for this project, I can select the one I want to use on the front of the invitation, click and drag it to a spot on the invitation in the main pane, and watch as it appears there. (See figure 9.3.)

At this point the photo will probably not be the right size or in the right spot. Do not worry. All your editing tools are still available. (More on this in a minute.) Not only are the standard tools available, there are now additional tools you can use to enhance the creativity of the project. If you want, you can click on the "Add something" button. You'll see a menu showing such things as text, shapes, etc. It is fun just to click on this and follow all the submenus that appear one after the other. I think it is amazing to see all the possibilities.

The "Effects" button offers antique, black and white, freehand painting, plus additional information explaining other options such as filters. The "Edges" button gives you choices such as different sizes and shapes, softness, and customization, and it offers help and options. You can even decide to add some additional images "at the last minute" by scanning in something or grabbing it off the camera. This means you are not limited to the images that are already on your computer.

What happens if you suddenly realize that it is more of a priority to make up the calendar with family photos and birthdates than it is finish the invitation? Go back to the "Create a project" button and start on something else. The first project is saved on the lower tray along with the images that you selected before. If you want to add more images or projects, it only means scrolling through this bar to find what you want.

A moment ago I mentioned that all of the familiar standard editing tools are still available and that this was significant. Why is this so? Imagine you have just returned from your skiing holiday in St. Moritz and want to send everyone a "card" showing you bouncing through the powder. You do not want to go through 200 images, name and edit each one, place them in albums, and then go to "Create a project." Right now all you want to do is send this one fabulous card. With all of the editing tools to the left on the "Common Tasks" bar or above on the toolbar, you do not have to wait until all the other photographs are edited. (Having given you this little "trick," I am of course a bit worried that you will ignore all the fine organizational information that I stressed in the earlier chapters. But I guess I'll have to trust you—and it is no longer my business.)

I started with Picture It! for several reasons. I think that it gives a wonderful and easy approach to having fun with your photographs. In addition, the "Companion Guide" is complete and well written. I have just given you an idea of a few things you can do. Play with the program itself or go directly to the guide for your step-by-step instructions for many more projects.

Jasc After Shot

If you recall, this program starts with a PowerPoint presentation explaining many of the things it can do and also how to do them. You can also check the user's guide for these directions, but I think it is nice to see where the menus and buttons are for each task suggested. In going through both of these helpful tools, I was struck by the fact that the real emphasis of this particular program is on creating a variety of image manipulations rather than everyday projects such as calendars, invitations, labels, etc.

All the programs covered in this book can add text, upload images, and send them as e-mail attachments. After Shot seems to specialize in turning images into movies, slide shows, stitched images, and Web pages. It can also add audio to these projects. It really emphasizes the computer as a tool with its own unique, creative slant.

Stitching

One of the terms I have used before in this book is "stitching." Stitching is the term used to describe putting two or more photographs together to form one panoramic view or collage of images. I think this is a useful and fun editing tool. Therefore, this is the project I will use to illustrate one of the excellent features of Jasc After Shot.

I am sure we have all stood on top of a tall building or a mountain pass and wanted to capture the vistas in front of us.

151

But a camera cannot see all the subtleties that our eyes can. Color, perspective, and range are limited. Even in the "panoramic" mode, a camera has limitations. Stitching solves the problem, but you must first decide "on site" that this is something you will want to do, and you must take *all* the photographs you will need to complete the project *correctly*. Remember the saying, "garbage in, garbage out."

If you plan to stitch images together, it is best to have your camera on a tripod so that it is steady and at a constant level for each shot. This may not be realistic, as most of us are not even interested in carrying a large camera and camera bag, much less carrying one more piece of equipment like a tripod. The first answer is to brace the camera against your body as you stand in one place. Alternatively, keep checking the Internet and the digital photography magazines, because specialty items are coming on the market all the time. (As I write this, one of the latest is a "dual function table pod." It is lightweight, inexpensive, and small enough to fit in a camera bag. It acts as a small tripod and a single-leg monopod.)

Assuming you are not using this new device, here is another tip that I always recommend for people doing a pan with a video camera. It also works well for this project. Point your feet towards the place where you will finish your pan. Then "wind-up" counterclockwise to the spot where you want to begin. By doing this you are in an "unstable" position for the briefest amount of time, and you get steadier as you "unwind." For your last photograph you will be as solid as a rock.

Other important points: hold the camera at the same level as you move around the axis, and overlap each image by as much as 50 percent. This is not to say that the "stitching" tool will not work if you do not follow these guidelines. However, it will make it a bit easier for the program to do its job if you help it as much as possible.

To help you understand what you will need to do when taking your own photographs, After Shot provides a series of images with which to practice the stitching technique. (This is very clever.) Open the After Shot program and notice the group of images in the large, main pane. Scroll towards the bottom of these "Sample Images" and find the six photographs that look like an island scene. They are labeled "Stitch 1.jpg," etc., for your convenience. Highlight these images and select them. As they are not contiguous—as yours will be, of course—I hold down the "Control" key (Ctrl) to select all six. (See figure 9.4.)

The directions in the user's guide say to either click on the folder "Stitches," which you will find either on the menu to the left (under the After Shot folder), or on the menu bar under "Tools." Even though I had used a proper CD to load this program onto my computer, I did not have the "Stitches" folder on the left and needed to go to the menu bar to find this tool. Be prepared to be flexible.

Once you do click on "Stitch," a new window will open with the six practice images visible. **Remember they may not be in the correct order**. That means that you will need to click and drag the images to their proper positions, moving from left to right (lower number to higher number). Now this is not my group of photographs, and unfortunately I have not had a chance to visit this lovely place. Therefore I have no idea whether the walkway is in the middle of the huts or at either end. When I place the cursor over one of the images, I do not get any information.

So this is what to do. Go back to the group of sample photos and look at each one (and its name) to determine which image is number one, two, three, etc. The other way to get this under control is to remember that the images overlap each other. Look at each one and see which ones have similar views. Does

Figure 9.4

Click here for the
"Stitch..." tool.

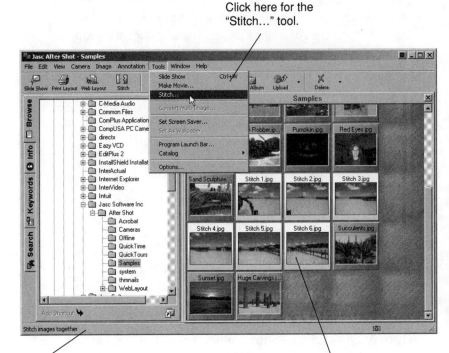

This bar confirms the
task you want to do.

Every image is named, and the ones
you will use are highlighted. In this
case the images are named correctly
and shot in order.

this seem like a big puzzle? Well yes, in some ways, but it does
teach you a valuable lesson. If you take your photographs in
order (contiguously), you should not have this problem.
Also, if you create a proper overlap, you can figure these things
out more easily. Finally, if you realize later that there is one
more part of the view that you want to include, that is fine.
You will be able to piece it all together in the correct order
later.

Once everything is lined up, you should notice that there are
two buttons to the left of the stitch image window. The lower

Figure 9.5

The Stitch button with the
Options button underneath

After
selecting
your
options,
click on
the Stitch
button.

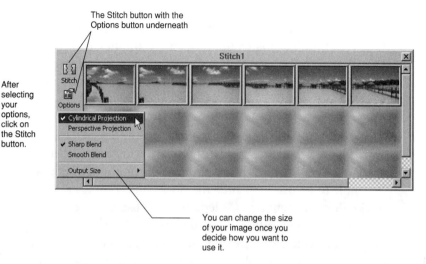

You can change the size
of your image once you
decide how you want to
use it.

one is "Options." Depending on the type of view you shot
and how well you actually captured the images, you can use
the selections in "Options" to optimize your final results. (See
figure 9.5.)

Your first option is to do a "Perspective Projection" or a
"Cylindrical Projection." The user's guide describes each of
these very well. The first type of projection is best for narrow to
medium horizontal views or vertical views. The concern in
using this format is that if the pan is wider, the edges of the
finished stitched image will look warped. The second
projection is best for views that are wide but not really tall
(a harbor scene with boats shot at a distance). In this case the
vertical lines will be fine, but horizontal lines might bend.
Needless to say, this is something you need to play with a bit.

The next step is to select "Smooth Blend" or a "Sharp Blend." If
your images are lined up pretty well, a smooth blend is a good
choice. It softens the images as it blends them together, and it
will correct for changes in exposures. Most of the time, this is

the "blend" to choose. If you have really messed up (and I am sorry to be so blunt) then you will need to do a sharp blend. What I mean by messing up is that the images are askew and things really do not match up. As its name implies, the transitions in this mode will be sharper, as will the contrast in brightness between the separate images. Again, try it out and judge for yourself.

The last option is determining the size of your finished image. If you want to send an e-mail or put something on the Web, this should be "Small." The resolution may not be as good, but the whole thing uses very little memory and is produced quickly. The next choice is "Medium." You use a little more memory, and the results are usually just fine. "Large" and "Very Large" will use much more memory, as they produce an image with a much higher resolution. It will take time to make a large or very large image, and it is not something that most of your friends will be able to download through their normal Internet connection.

So go ahead and check off the options you want to use for this practice session or use the preselected ones. Then click on the "Stitch" button.

Stitching takes time. You can either watch the blue bar at the bottom of the window to see exactly where the program is in the process, or you can work on something else while this is happening. The "Stitch" program will continue to run in the background. When it is finished, there is a new window that shows the *almost* final image. Notice that there is a white dashed line that is moving around the perimeter of the photograph. This is the suggested crop line. In a sharp blend, this line might be more extreme, but for this example the selected images did fit together well. If you do want to follow the suggested cropping, just click on the "Crop" icon on the tool bar. If you change your mind, click on "Undo," but the "suggested" crop

Figure 9.6

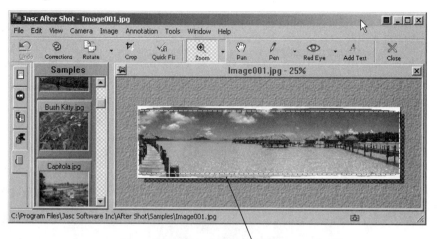

Here you can see the new stitched image along with the suggested (and only) crop lines available.

seems to be your only crop option. (See figure 9.6.) Having played with the sample images, I could not resist trying this for myself. Check out the next four figures (9.7a, 9.7b, 9.7c, and 9.7d) to see my results. It really was fun and easy.

There are more things you can do with this new photograph. Play around a bit with the "Add Text" feature. If you are really adventuresome, try clicking on the "Pen" button. (I can never get this one to work for me very well, but then again I am not very artistic.)

As I mentioned before, and as you can see for yourself, each program has its own strengths and weaknesses. In some ways choosing an image-editing program is similar to your first step in this process—choosing the camera that you wanted to buy. You had to think about exactly how you wanted to use the hardware. Now you can start to see some of the major differences in the software.

Figure 9.7a

I could not resist trying this myself, so here are my
images of the famous Flat Irons of Boulder, Colorado
taken at sunrise.

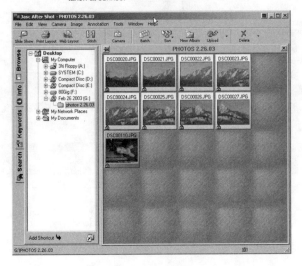

Figure 9.7b

To stitch these images, I click
on "Tool" from the menu bar
and then click on "Stitch…"

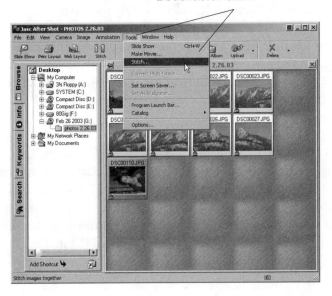

Figure 9.7c

First I need to line up my images in the correct order.

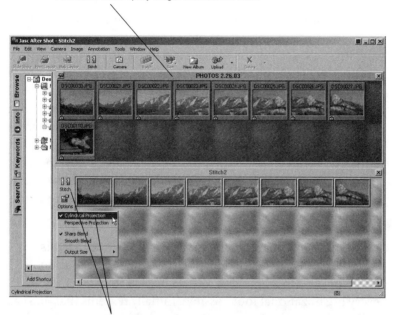

After selecting from the options drop down menu,
click on "Stitch."

Figure 9.7d

The finished product with the suggested crop lines.

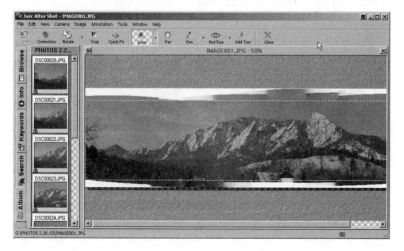

ACDSee

ACD Systems has created a program that is known as a very powerful organizing tool. Every image can be catalogued with more information than most of us could ever understand or use. Images can be grabbed from anywhere, including stills from video. These photos can then be reorganized one at a time or in batches and moved from one folder to another quite easily. Audio features and text are added with just a few clicks. And with all this organization, one can use the most basic information to search and find these images instantly. As with the program After Shot, there is an emphasis on multimedia first and then the basic tasks of printing and e-mailing. In fact that is how the software is advertised on the cover of the user guide, "The #1 Choice to Manage, Enhance and Share Your Digital Images—Fast!"

However in this chapter the question is, what else can this software do? ACDSee obviously makes the images look good, and it puts them where they should be—in this case after using every organizational tool possible. Initially it seems that one has to buy additional software that is compatible with ACDSee to get those additional "project" tools. Having checked all the software currently available from the ADC Systems Web site, it is evident that all of these programs compliment the strengths of the main system. They do not add an easy approach to creative projects. In other words, if you want to do the same things in a better and faster way, there is ACD software that can help you to do that.

There are some tools in the main program that offer "limited" projects. In the ACDSee work area, called the "Browse Window," there are two icons on the main toolbar that really answer it all. One is labeled "Create," and the other is labeled "Extra." If you click on the "Create" button there are five choices: "Wallpaper," "Archive," "Contact Sheet," "Print Contact Sheet," and "HTML." The "Extra" icon only offers "Slide Show."

This does not mean that you are stuck with a program that is limited to printing, creating slide shows and Web pages,

160

editing, and cataloging. But you will need to approach the other projects you would like to do in a more roundabout way.

Invitations—Another Approach

As an example, let's say you want to make an invitation. It will be a simple one of double thickness, folded on the left side, with an image on the outside and the information on the right-hand inside page. The thing to do is to find an image to use for the front of the invitation and copy it to a Word document. It should be placed in the upper left side of the page and fill one quarter of the page (approximately 4″ × 5.5″—you can estimate with the ruler and the scroll bar). Now here is the trick—rotate the image 180 degrees. Next reset your margins so you are working in the lower right quarter of the page. Fill in the information for your event.

Now print out this page. Fold the page in half horizontally and in half vertically. Your invitation should now have the image on the outside with the information on the right inside. I know it sounds complicated, but all that is happening is that you are following the same techniques that were used to print books, etc., in the past.

There are also special programs that you can buy to make labels, T-shirts, and more. The point is that you have the images, and with the additional software, you can create many projects. Remember that the ACDSee software has many important features that you will find very useful. It is a question of recognizing your needs when selecting a program.

Photoshop Elements

Adobe Photoshop Elements is first and foremost a painting and drawing program that is designed to transform or manipulate images. Professionals use software like this to create the advertisements you see in magazines. It also has an impressive array of photo-editing tools. This is exactly what you want to have if you are trying to "redo" your photographs.

However, once again this is a problem if your goal is just to have a quick way to do projects. The software is truly impressive in the way it does its job. But that does not really help you if you want to make a calendar or print out announcements and invitations.

There is a difference, though, between this program and the ones mentioned previously that have limited "built in" creative tools. Photoshop Elements can produce special effects, layers of images and text, multiple image layouts, and much more. This means that you can take your images and then enhance them in such a way that they can be used to create projects that look truly professional.

Cards

The example I will use to illustrate this is to make a card using some photographs and adding interesting text. This will also involve using the "Layer" tool or palette, so it will give you a bit of experience with this part of the program. Technically, Photoshop Elements can produce an image with up to 8,000 layers, but I will keep this project simple—maybe six to eight layers.

The first thing to do is to create a new document that will be the "project." To do this go to "File" on the menu bar and click on "New." The window you see will ask you to name your project. Let's make this one "Winter Birthday Invitation." You also need to pick the dimensions of the finished card. If you are not sure how to handle this, either use one of the default measurements or measure something around you, like a greeting card or medium-size pad of paper and use those dimensions. The number of pixels is also a bit confusing, but 300 dpi (or the default) is usually safe unless your are making a very large invitation—in which case you better be sure you can get envelopes to match!

I want to use color for this card, but I will start with "Transparent" for my layers. Check the appropriate boxes and then click the "OK" button.

162

I will use several tools that have not been discussed before. To find different palettes you need to click on "Window" on the menu bar. All the palettes are there and the ones to select for this project are "Layers" and "Swatches." They sit as separate windows on the work area, and you should just move them to a convenient spot. The other tools I will use are the paintbrush and the gradient tools, which are on the left side of the main window in the toolbox. I will also need the "Text" tool (fourth icon down on the right side) and will pick out some "clip art" or photographs from a folder on my desktop. (See figure 9.8.)

Figure 9.8

As this project will use several layers, you want to have the "Layers" palette open for this.

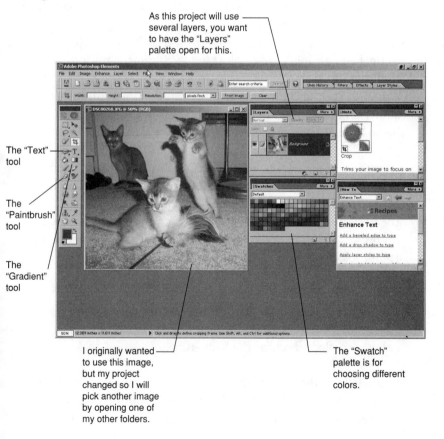

The "Text" tool

The "Paintbrush" tool

The "Gradient" tool

I originally wanted to use this image, but my project changed so I will pick another image by opening one of my other folders.

The "Swatch" palette is for choosing different colors.

Another thing to do will be changing the different levels of "opacity" in the card. A way of describing opacity is that an almost transparent layer does not block the layer beneath it and is a very low number on the opacity scale. If a layer has a high opacity number, then it will be almost opaque and block what is underneath it. This is true unless other tools are used to take some of the image away (such as "Dissolve" or "Erase"). In this program if you specify "Transparent," the opacity setting makes no difference.

Getting back to our card, first you have to create a background layer. To select a color, click on "Window" on the menu bar and select "Swatches," and while you are at it, select "Layers," too. Then move these new windows to the right side of the work space. From the "Swatches" palette, click on "Pure Blue Violet" (one of my favorites) for the foreground and "White" (default) as the background. These colors are visible at the bottom of the toolbox. If you want a different background color, click on the box in the background and pick your new color from the grid shown in the new window. Do not forget to click on the "OK" button when you are done. (See figure 9.9.)

If you have opened this program and you are following along with each step, you are probably worried that the first window for the card appears in a checkerboard pattern—I certainly was the first time I saw this. Let's get rid of it. The sixth icon down on the left in the toolbox looks like a paintbrush (the one to the right looks like a pencil). When you click on this icon you have various choices on the options bar. To make life easier I suggest making the brush large and fuzzy and changing the pixel setting to a large number. By holding down the left mouse button and moving the cursor around the entire card, you now have the color you selected set for the background.

Next click on the "Gradient" tool (fifth icon down, right side). Again there are a number of choices on the option bar. Leave it on the first one—a gradual fade from the foreground color to

Figure 9.9

For this project the
first layer is going to
be the image.

The second
layer is the
background.

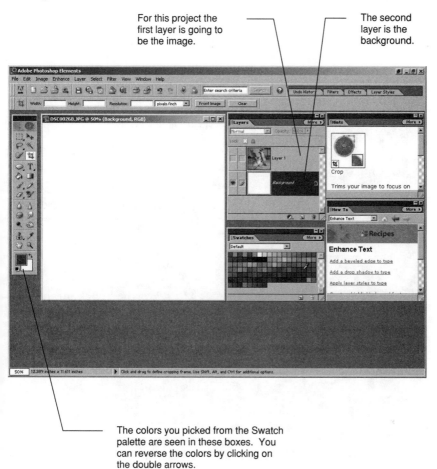

The colors you picked from the Swatch
palette are seen in these boxes. You
can reverse the colors by clicking on
the double arrows.

the background color. If you do decide to click on the down
arrow to the right, you can select from a number of other color
and design variations. If you click on "Edit," just to the right of
that, you get a large window called the "Gradient Editor." This
gives even more details about type, smoothness, and
controllable color variation. And there is always the "More"
button if you think something is missing! Once you have made
your primary selection, there are several other possibilities—the

Figure 9.10

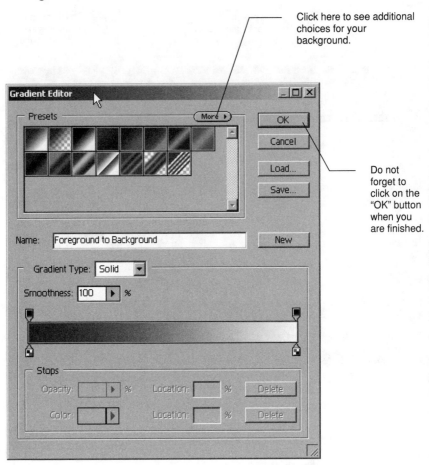

Click here to see additional choices for your background.

Do not forget to click on the "OK" button when you are finished.

gradient of color can be done in either a linear, radial, angular, reflected, or diamond pattern. (See figure 9.10.)

By now I think you get the point. This is just one of many tools at your disposal—and this is actually one of the simplest. Why not play with some "Gradient" options when you get a chance? Right now it is time to finish the birthday invitation.

You have a background, and it is time to add the feeling of winter lights to the card. This will be layer two. First let's make the lights white. Go to the bottom of the toolbox and click the little "Reverse" arrows on the right of the color boxes. Now the white box is in front and the blue behind. On the menu bar click on "Layer," then click on "New," and from the next submenu, click on "Layer." The new window tells you that you are now working on layer three, and it allows you to change the opacity from 100 percent to the 33 percent setting that I think is the one to use for this card. (See figure 9.11.)

Next click on the brush tool and select a soft brush. The "size" of the lights is determined by the next option ("Size") and is

Figure 9.11

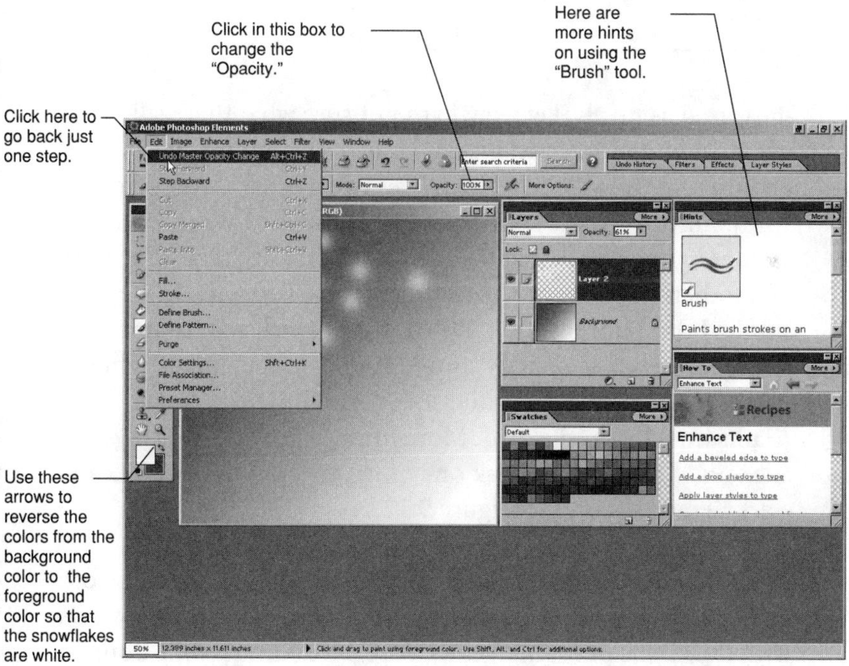

Click in this box to change the "Opacity."

Here are more hints on using the "Brush" tool.

Click here to go back just one step.

Use these arrows to reverse the colors from the background color to the foreground color so that the snowflakes are white.

Figure 9.12

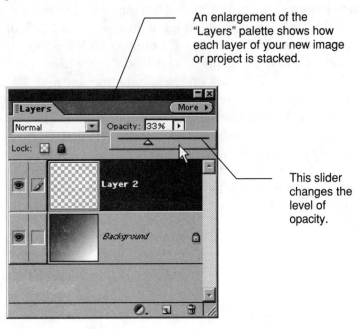

An enlargement of the "Layers" palette shows how each layer of your new image or project is stacked.

This slider changes the level of opacity.

measured as pixels. Let's say I am not sure what this really means. I find it easier to pick a reasonable number, like 90, and then see how large a circle I get when I place the cursor (my paintbrush) in a spot on the card. Maybe I want several sizes of lights. If so, I just make a few of one size and some more of another. With 33-percent opacity, these lights are rather subtle. If I do not like that, I go to the "Layer" palette and change the level of opacity using the box on the upper right side of the window. As I move the slider right or left, it shows the results directly on the card. More importantly, I can always just click on "Edit" and go back one move, several moves, or I can start all over again. (See figure 9.12.)

The next layer will have some art. From my folders I can select something like stylized mountains or skiers. (You can buy CDs with hundreds of art images that are part of the public domain, meaning they are free. If you are going to do a lot of projects, it is a good idea to have several resources.) To add this layer, go to "File" on the menu bar, click on "Import," and select what you want to import and from where.

The next thing is to type in the message. Select the "Text" tool from the toolbar. Then go to the options bar and decide on the usual things such as format, fonts, placement, etc. You also have to decide whether your lettering will run horizontally or vertically. (The text will not "wrap around," so you need to press the "Enter" key for each new line.) Things can now be as simple or as fancy as you would like. If you want to distort the text, you must first highlight it. Then there are several icons on the options bar from which to choose. If you pick "Warp," the next window offers fifteen styles of warps, and after choosing one of these, you get to decide the percentage of "Bend," "Horizontal Distortion," and "Vertical Distortion" you want. All I can say about this is that it has really helped me to have the "Undo" and the "Cancel" button. Sometimes I can get carried away!

Just because you have one bit of text on the card, it does not mean that you cannot add another layer either in another color or in a different direction. This is where the idea of multiple layers makes the project look professional and also makes the production a lot of fun.

Finally think about adding a special photograph. Click on "Layer" to start one more. Then click on "File" from the menu bar and "Open" to find the image you want to use. You will now see that photograph on the "Layer" palette. Drag it to the card. Click on "Image" from the menu bar, then "Transform," and then "Free Transform" from the submenu. (See figure 9.13.) At this point you can change the size by horizontal and vertical percentages. You can also rotate the image so it is slanted any way that you like. You can also move it around so it sits in a certain area on the card.

You now have a special card, and the rest is up to you. (See figure 9.14.) You can save it as you would any other document

Figure 9.13

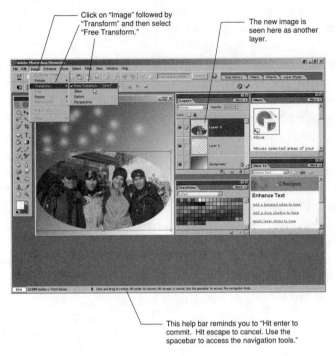

Click on "Image" followed by "Transform" and then select "Free Transform."

The new image is seen here as another layer.

This help bar reminds you to "Hit enter to commit. Hit escape to cancel. Use the spacebar to access the navigation tools."

Figure 9.14

The finished product with the text added as the last layer.

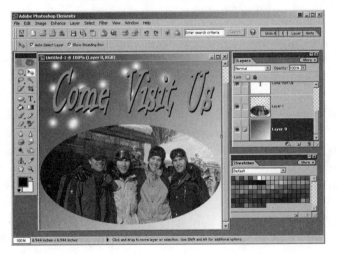

and print it out. You can send it as an attachment to an e-mail or use it on a Web site. If you have special software, you can print it out and put it on a T-shirt or coffee mug. This may not have been as easy as simply clicking on a button to create a project. But, to my mind you now have a much more interesting finished product.

The Final Analysis

Now you have seen some of the different projects that all four programs can do. Some programs make it easier than others to do certain projects. As I mentioned at the beginning of the chapter, there will be trade-offs if you are using only one particular program. My answer to this problem is to ask a rather simple question. Why have only one image-editing program on your computer? Let's say you like the way Photoshop Elements edits your images, but find it easier to do simple projects using Picture It!. Forgetting the expense, why not have both or all the programs? You can do your editing in one program and then have it sitting in its folder (neatly catalogued by still another program, ACDSee). When you want to make a calendar or a birthday card all you have to do is open Picture It! and pick the project you want to do. After all, you can import an image from anywhere. And what about After Shot? Well, in the second week of your training, why not make a movie?!?

10

Chapter 10
Points Still to Be Discussed

The Programs

The purpose of this book is to give you an introduction to editing your digital photographs. I believe I have done this in the past few chapters with an explanation of how to use the basic editing tools of four different image-editing programs. In fact there are dozens of image-editing programs—one of which was part of the bundle of things that came with your digital camera. If you already have an editing program, is it necessary to buy another one? Obviously, I think it is. It all comes down to one of the first questions I asked at the beginning of the book. Do you know what you want to do with your photographs? This was an important question in choosing the correct camera, and it is just as important in choosing your digital image-editing software.

I have already discussed the advantages and disadvantages associated with the four programs. Some can edit quickly, but very simply. You have minimal control over the edits, and you will have trouble getting back to your original image. But you will not have to spend a lot of time creating something that you can enjoy. Some programs help you organize the images easily, and can show you a tremendous number of your photographs very quickly. This speed and organization might be all that you want (especially if you take 300 photographs every time you go on vacation). Some programs have more advanced editing tools, but do not help you create even the simplest projects (unless you enjoy jumping through hoops). Two things to keep in mind: you need to decide what is most important to you, and you are not limited to using only one program.

The Specialty Packages

At the moment, there are several companies that are trying to make this whole process much simpler. Kodak, Hewlett-Packard, Fuji, Casio, and other manufacturers have developed systems that combine a camera with a docking station (or USB direct connection) along with their own special software. What this means is that after taking your photographs, you place the camera in the docking station, press a button, and have everything transferred to your computer. While this is happening, the company's software opens to its viewing program automatically. Now you have your images right in front of you. Some of the programs even let you name your images before uploading, or the program arranges the photographs for you by date or other factors. In many cases, including the Canon, Sony, and Panasonic systems, you can have a connection that goes directly to a printer, PDA, or DVD recorder.

Kodak and HP use well-developed software that makes it very easy for you to do things like e-mailing and printing. I am sure you have all seen the advertisements for these two systems on television. But you should be aware that the cameras themselves are considered to be at the lower end of the market. This means they have limited features and megapixels. The docking stations are usually sold separately (currently for approximately $80). However, the docking station also acts as a battery charger, and that is a nice feature. In addition these systems have their own Web sites for uploading large batches of images. This means you can have a place to which you can direct your family and friends when they want to see *all* the photographs.

At this time Kodak is using a familiar approach. The company is following the same philosophy of photography that George Eastman pioneered. Eastman sold his box cameras for very little money. He knew that people would need film, and selling the film was the way to make real money. The Kodak digital system is supposed to work with the majority of printers, however, for some reason, in each case it seems to require the use of Kodak paper in order to make quality prints.

Of course Hewlett-Packard's system also works with all printers, but I think it works best with its own. There are even specialty HP printers designed just for digital photographs. The

HP system also has features that allow you to connect the docking station to a television.

One caveat: By the time you are reading these paragraphs some of this technology may have changed. For this reason I strongly recommend checking out the most recent digital photography magazines and going to Web sites such as cnet.com for the latest information and comparisons.

Scanning Images into the Computer

When you are working in your editing program, you have to decide where you are going to get your image. One of the options is to scan an image into your computer. This seems to be easy enough, but, as with most things in life, there are several things to know and consider before you do this. A scanner is like a copying machine. You place something on the flatbed, press a button, and the image is recognized and sent to your computer. It does this one line at a time. There are several types of scanners, and when thinking about buying one, you must once again consider your needs. If you are getting a scanner to load all your 35-millimeter film photographs into the computer, there are scanners that are designed for this particular task. Most of us need something a little more versatile and so a "flatbed" scanner would be our first choice. This way we can use it for photos, documents, newspaper articles, forms, and anything else you want.

The main points to consider when buying a scanner include resolution, color depth, and use. Most people think that bigger is better. The reality is that the less expensive scanners can probably handle any job you would want to do.

The average resolution on these low-end machines is 300 dpi (dots per inch). This is the optical resolution. The reason for the obsession with "dpi" is that the higher the resolution, the greater the detail. Another way of saying this is that if you have a small image (such as a 4″ × 6″ photograph) and want to turn it into a large print, you need the greater number of dots per inch or the image will be very blurred. (A way around this is to have the capability of changing the dpi setting of your scanner before starting the actual scan. That would be one reason for getting a scanner with a bit of flexibility.) However, if your printer only prints at 300dpi, there is no reason to even attempt going from a small print to a larger one.

The other reason for setting a more "reasonable" dpi setting is that the higher the resolution, the larger the file. This means it will take up more space on your hard drive and take much longer to upload and download. There is an equation that helps you to figure out exactly how many megabytes of space are used with different dpi settings, but it is rather complicated. (That means I do not really want to get into all this here, and if you want to see the figures please check Appendix B.) The calculation usually shows that increasing the dpi is a geometrical rather than an arithmetic progression.

Color depth refers to how many colors can be digitized. It is measured by the number of bits per pixel. Less expensive scanners are usually 24-bit and the expensive scanners are 36-bit. In real terms, a 24-bit scanner can digitize more than 16 million colors and a 36-bit scanner can digitize billions of colors. In fact the human eye can only see the 16 million colors. Given this information, why choose the 36-bit scanner? The reason is that if you are working professionally, it makes a difference to be able to "see" the variation of color in dark areas or the variation in very colorful areas. For most of us, the obvious choice is the less expensive machine.

Which brings us to the last point, how do you want to use your scanner? There are so many to choose from and it is not just a question of cost, but also the amount of space that you have available on your desk. Flatbed scanners take up a lot of space, but they are versatile. Photographic scanners can basically do one thing, but they do it very well. My personal solution to the whole problem was to buy a "combination" machine. It is a color printer, color copier, color scanner, and color fax machine. It is quick, it is efficient, it takes up less room than even two devices, and it cost less than my digital camera.

Printers

The chances are that you already own or are going to buy an inkjet printer because of its cost. Laser printers, within a reasonable price range, produce black, white, and grayscale printing. Inkjet printers do a very good job of printing photographic images and text. The color is good and everything becomes even better when using the "best" print setting and the highest-quality paper for the project at hand.

The variables for a printer are resolution, speed, size of paper, and, of course, color. Most of the affordable inkjet printers will offer 300 dpi or 600 dpi. Either one should be able to handle most of your needs. Speed is something that is relative. Most of the time we think that everything is moving too slowly (unless it is our vacation). While things have improved, color printing takes time, and there is no way around that. The size of the paper is also a factor to consider if you want to print larger photographs or legal documents. If you really do not need to do this a lot, you might want to go to a specialty print shop if you want a larger image. It is a better idea than spending money for a feature that will not get much use.

Finally there is the question of color. Most of us have printers that have two cartridges—one is black and the other is "color." My new printer has four cartridges, as the "color" cartridge is now separated into three cartridges, one for each of the main colors. For high-quality photographic printing, you can buy printers with seven or more color cartridges.

Once again there is nothing that says you can only have one printer. Perhaps you might want to consider having a regular printer for your text printing and one of the specialty printers for photographs. The prices are coming down, and this arrangement might be the answer to all your printing needs.

Sharing Photographs

There are a variety of ways to share your photographs. If you have a lot of images, you can save them on CDs and send them to all your friends. If you have just a few photographs, you can e-mail them. But you need to be careful about how many you are sending and their size (in kilobytes): it also would help if you know whether your recipient has a high-speed Internet line. (There is no faster way to ruin a friendship than to send a lot of large images to someone who is using a dial-up connection. After their computer crashes the second time, watch out!) The alternative is to have a Web page or to upload your images to a photo-sharing service.

Each editing program describes several ways of creating your own Web page. This is an excellent way not only to share your photographs, but also to provide information about your "goings on" to family and friends. It allows people to keep in touch in a different way than e-mailing. This is especially important for some of the nontechnical or older members of the family who might find downloading attachments difficult. It also solves the problem of a slower Internet connection.

One other way of sharing your photographs is to join one of the many "image-sharing" Web sites. It seems that there is one associated with each of the camera companies (Sony has one called Image Station), and each of the Internet Service Providers (Microsoft uses a service called MSN Photos). Often there is a limited amount of space given to your "account." You can make this a private site that requires a password, or open it to the public. You can create different albums, each with its own password. This way your family can view your new apartment or college friends, while your friends can see the wild "house-warming" party they all attended. All of these are good choices and worth exploring.

In Conclusion

There are obviously many more things that I could talk about concerning digital-image editing, software programs, hardware and "plug-ins," printing images, special projects, and archiving photographs. Please remember that the concept of this book is to help you through your first week—to serve as your introduction to many aspects of digital photography. The reason this book exists is that several of my friends came to me and said, "I just got a digital camera. I know how to take pictures, and I can get the pictures onto the computer, but what do I do with them now?" For all of my friends, family, and especially for you—the person who bought this book—I hope I have helped answer that question.

11

Chapter 11
Where is My *Step-by-Step* Guide?

This series of books, *The First Week,* is noted for several things, not the least of which is Chapter 11, your step-by-step guide for performing all the tasks mentioned in the first 10 chapters. The reason this chapter existed in the first place was because I wrote a manual to teach my 85-year-old mother how to use her personal computer. It was 10 chapters long, and while she really enjoyed reading it "in bed," she said to me, "Can't you just tell me where I should point the cursor and what I should do with it?" In thinking about it, I realized that when businesses had problems they had a financial "bail out"—Chapter 11. It seemed reasonable that Mother should also have a bail out. So she received her own type of Chapter 11—an information bail out.

Why am I telling you all this? Simply because I will not be writing a step-by-step guide for this book, as I did for the other books in the series.

There are two reasons for this. The first is that the printed material, tutorials, and "tips" that come with each of the four image-editing programs usually cover the one, two, threes of each tool you will be using. Often the explanations are quite good, but sometimes they are a bit difficult to understand. That is why I have tried to simplify the most important features of each program in this book. The second reason is that it would be too difficult to write an outline of each of the most important features of four digital image editing programs, and then put it all in one chapter. I would imagine that doing so would mean that Chapter 11 would be longer than the first 10 chapters of this book combined.

So if you were looking forward to having a step-by-step guide to turn to, I apologize if I have disappointed you. However, I hope you have found the information I have chosen to include to be interesting, informative, and even a bit amusing.

Appendices

Appendix A
Troubleshooting and Many of Your Additional Questions

Why do I need to edit my photographs?
The easy answer is that you do not have to edit your photographs. You may have taken wonderful images and be happy with the initial results. Congratulations, as you are a better photographer than most of us! But since this is the first week, I am assuming that you are still getting used to your new camera and will need to make some adjustments to your photographs. Isn't that why you bought this book? Plus, even if your photographs are wonderful, you will still want to organize them, and the programs discussed in this book will help you to do this.

Why do I need more than one program?
The reason I suggest owning more than one image-editing program is that each of the programs seems to have its own special attributes. One organizes very well, another has templates that make projects easy, and another is the ultimate image-editing tool. They are not expensive, so why not have more than one?

Why should I use an "automatic fix" tool sometimes, but not all the time?
It is always a good idea to try the simplest correction first. If you do not like it, you can always start over. I also recommend the idea of trying a gamma correction if you think your black and white levels are fine and just want to change the middle tones. In some cases, however, the auto fix will not help at all. It might be too basic a tool for the number of things that need to be changed. That is why you have all the other tools for correcting your image.

Why doesn't the "Undo" feature work all the time?
It is not that the "Undo" tool does not work. It is that in some programs it will only go back by one step—your most recent

correction. If you forget to undo a change immediately, you might make three or four changes, not like them, and then have a bit of a mess as you cannot get back to your starting point. That is one reason in favor of always working with a copy rather than your original image.

Why should I make a copy of my photographs before editing them?
See the answer to the question above.

Why do the colors look different in different photos, even when I've taken all the pictures in the same house at the same time?
While your camera will try to correct for changes in light sources with an automatic setting for the white balance, it does not always work. Each type of lightbulb gives off a different tone or tint. Incandescent bulbs give off a yellowish tint, while fluorescent bulbs are bluish. Colors in photos are also affected by the flash and whether the room is dim or filled with sunlight.

Why do the images and colors look different on my prints than they did on my monitor?
Your monitor is capable of producing an unlimited number of colors—even more than your eyes can perceive. Your printer is much more limited in its color spectrum. Also, if you have a very basic printer, all the colors are combined in one ink cartridge. This means it can reproduce even fewer colors than a printer with multiple color cartridges.

Why is it that sometimes I can store lots of images on my memory card and sometimes it is full after I only shoot a few photographs?
All of this depends on the resolution setting on your camera. The higher the resolution, the fewer images you can store. Each image is a set of pixels and the more you use for each image, the more memory space each photo takes up on your card. That is the reason for either carrying several memory cards or recognizing that e-mail images do not need a lot of pixels.

How do I know what resolution to use for taking a picture, for printing a picture, and for sending a picture over the Internet?
This is a good question. If you want to take a photograph of something "special," you will probably want to make a reasonable-size print of the image. This means using the highest resolution possible to produce a really nice 8″ × 10″ print. However if you do this, you will use more of your memory space and will be able to fit fewer images on one card. Once again, your choice of setting depends on how you will use your images. For sending an image over the Internet or creating a Web page, you should use the lowest resolution on your camera because it will take less time to upload and download. This means your friends will not get angry and refuse to download any of your pictures.

Why do my friends get angry with me when I send them a set of photographs that I think they would like to see and that I think are great?
This is answered in the two questions above. The fact is, that the larger the image file, the longer it will take to download. If you are using a high-speed line, you can upload everything quickly. If the recipients have dial-up connections, your large-resolution image will crash their computers when they are trying to download it. One solution is to use a private image service or Web site for your folders. Then your family and friends can see thumbnail (small) views and just enlarge the ones of interest. (Which also addresses another aspect of this question. Just because you think the photographs are great and want everyone to see them, does not mean your friends really care about your New Year's Eve party. They might feel you should have invited them instead of just sending photos!)

Why do I see jagged lines when I make my photographs larger?
Each photograph is really a number of little squares. Think about the images you see in newspapers, comic books, or Roy Lichtenstein paintings. When enlarged you can see all the individual dots. Your images look like "normal" photographs at

186

a certain size. When the same number of squares (pixels) must spread out to fill in a larger space, they do not do this very well. The result is jagged, stair-step lines, especially around the diagonal edges, which are called "jaggies."

Why do the colors seem blurred together and uneven when I enlarge my photograph?
This is similar to the problem of "jaggies" (see above). This effect is called "artifacts." It happens when the computer program tries to figure out what colors are needed to "fill in" the empty spaces created because the pixels "spread out."

Why do I get lines and streaks when I print my photographs?
As you are referring to your printed image, it is a hardware problem, and you need to check the printer settings and the ink cartridges.

How do I know if I should get a printer that is just for printing photographs?
New photo printers are available at very reasonable prices. Your inkjet printer will work nicely for most jobs, but it is limited because it probably has two cartridges—one black and the other "color." This means that the color cartridge is trying to combine all three colors to create your color image. A specialized printer usually has separate cartridges for the main colors. Some of these printers are so small and light that you can fit them in your camera bag. Then you can print $4'' \times 6''$ images immediately. In addition some manufacturers have developed new machines that produce much smaller dots. That means much higher print resolution for each photo.

How do I know if I should get a digital camera that is part of an integrated system?
This is hard for me to answer. Once again you need to think about how you want to use the camera and the quality of the camera you wish to buy. However, remember that just because

it is an integrated system, you are not limiting yourself. You are just making some tasks easier.

How do I keep from overloading my hard drive's memory with all my photo albums?

Storage is always a problem (especially at my house). But seriously, when we talk about storing digital photographs, here are some thoughts. First make sure you have gotten rid of all the images you do not need anymore. Then consider storing your images on CDs or CD-RWs (see the Glossary). Another solution is to buy an external storage device. This will also take care of many of your other computer storage needs.

I know I want to take some of the blue out of my photograph. What is the best way to do it?

Each of the editing programs has color correction. In some ways it is fun to slide the different controls from one side to the other to see just how bad you can make your mother-in-law look. From this experiment you will learn that color correction is really very delicate, and you need to make changes slowly and with moderation. However, to answer the question, you cannot just reduce the amount of blue to make the change. To get the proper correction, you also have to increase the red and the green. One of the best formulas I have seen for this is that if you decrease the blue by "x" amount, you need to increase the red and green by the same amount ("x") divided by two.

I did a red-eye correction but now my sister looks like an alien. What did I do wrong?

You forgot to leave a little bit of white in the center of the eyes. Look at yourself in the mirror and you will notice the little "glint" that we all have. I guess this is what makes us different from aliens.

What the hell is a gamma correction?

The direct answer is that this is the tool that changes the gray scale of your image. "Brightness" and "Contrast" tools work with the entire image equally—especially the black and white ends of the scale. "Gamma Correction" tools work on the area

in between the black and white. So if you look at your image and like the dark and light areas, but still feel that something is not right, the "Gamma Correction" tool should brighten up (or tone down) that center area of color.

I like taking pictures with my 35-millimeter camera, I do not want to buy a new camera, and I do not mind spending money having my film/slides processed. However, I do want to be able to edit my own images and e-mail them to friends. What do I do?
When you have your photographs processed, also have your images put on a CD. Then you can load it onto your computer and work with any one of the image-editing programs that you enjoy using.

I thought you were going to tell me how to store telephone numbers in my cell phone and how to program the clock on my VCR. What's the story?
Every cell phone is different, so if you are having trouble with yours and do not understand the user's manual, it would be

best to go back to the store and have one of the bright young people there show you what to do. (Make notes so that you will remember these directions in the future.) Alternatively, bring along your telephone directory or PDA so this young person can enter *all* your numbers. As for your VCR, find the little button on the machine that says "clock." Try pressing it and then playing with the up and down arrows nearby. If nothing happens or there is no "clock" button, sorry, this is way past my expertise.

How do I know when I have finished all the image editing I need to do?

This is my favorite question.

As Michelangelo supposedly said in response to Pope Julius II's questions concerning the completion of the Sistine Chapel, "It will be finished when it is done."

My answer to the question is, do not go overboard—especially in the beginning. Try printing some photographs or sending a few to yourself via e-mail. Then you can judge if you like what you see. Less is more. Just because you can clone, layer, paint, and swing the color wheel does not mean that you have to do it for every image. It is much more important that you spend the extra time organizing your photographs so you can find them in the future.

Appendix B
Formulas for Print Size, Resolution, Etc.

I know I said in an earlier chapter that I did not want to get into details about the formulas for things such as scanner resolution, amount of space needed on the hard disk for different size images, and how large a print you can produce based on the original number of pixels in the image. Some people really like seeing these kinds of equations and charts so I have added them here.

Note: This is not required reading for your first week of digital image editing!

Print Size

I would think that your most pressing question right now is, "I have just edited a photograph. How large a print can I make from this image?" Your printer may allow you to make a few changes to the standard settings, but it probably has three print "quality" settings. They are usually described as "Draft," "Normal," and "Best." The description does not help you, because it does not tell you the dpi(dots per inch) for each setting. However, what it usually means is that it is offering to print anywhere from 150 dpi on up.

When you bought your camera you considered the number of megapixels it could produce in an image. There is a reason for this. The higher the number of pixels in an image, the clearer the image will be when it is printed in a larger format. With a camera capable of a 3.0 to 3.3 megapixel image, you can have a nice clear 8″ × 10″ print. (This translates to an image that is described as "2048 × 1536" pixels or approximately a 3:2 ratio.) If you are only going to e-mail your images or place them on the Web, you do not need to have anything larger than "640 × 480" pixels. All of this is also referred to as "ppi," or pixels per inch. (By the way, I just checked the settings on my own camera to remind myself of the exact numbers. I normally shoot images that are "1280 × 960," as that setting produces a normal-size print and does not take up a lot of space on my memory card. Also my camera can be set to simultaneously take a 640 × 480 "separate" image for e-mailing. Therefore I have two options with one "click.")

In order to answer the question of how large of a print you can make, there are two things to consider. The first is what does it mean to have too few or two many pixels? If there are too few, a larger print size will be blurry. If there are a lot of pixels, you can print that large image, but if all your want is a 4″ × 6″ snapshot, you have not gained anything and you have used up memory card space. The second consideration is what your printer can produce. Try different settings and see what looks good to you.

For those of you who feel better seeing the actual numbers, here is a chart based on several of my many "user guides." It assumes you have a camera that can go up to 3.3 megapixels per image. ("What?" you say, "You are using a generic chart?" Of course I am. You did not actually expect me to do this math myself, did you?)

Print Size	Pixels for 200 dpi	Pixels for 300 dpi	Needed Camera Resolution
3.5 × 5	1000 × 700	1500 × 1050	1 megapixel
4 × 6	1200 × 800	1800 × 1200	1 megapixel
5 × 7	1400 × 1000	2100 × 1500	3 megapixels
8 × 10	2000 × 1600	3000 × 2400	3 megapixels
11 × 13	3400 × 2200	5100 × 3300	6 megapixels
13 × 19	3800 × 2600	5700 × 3900	10 megapixels

Scanners

Scanners copy an image and enter this image into your computer. You can then edit the image and print it. Of course the easiest approach would be if the photograph you wanted to scan was 300 dpi and the printer you wanted to use to produce the new image was set at 300 dpi, with the new image staying the same size as the original. If that is the case, there is no reason to worry about equations.

However, there is always the possibility that your original is a 4″ × 6″ image and you want to enlarge this to an 8″ × 10″ print. First you will need to scan the original image at a high resolution to ensure a good-quality print as your final result. I personally think experimentation is a good approach. As you already know, I usually try to avoid mathematical equations. For those who insist on "working it out," here is the equation for setting the correct scanner resolution.

$$\text{final dpi} \times \frac{\text{intended image width}}{\text{original image width}} = \text{Scanner Resolution}$$

I think an example always makes things like this easier to understand. Your image will be printed at 300 dpi. The original photograph is 4″ × 6″ and you want the new print to be 8″ × 10.″

$$300 \times \frac{8}{4} = 600$$

What this means is that you need to set your scanner to scan the original image at a 600 dpi resolution, so that the new image will be the same quality print as the original.

Note: If this does not work, I do not want you to send your complaints to me. All of the above is based on the information I received from Jonah, my new best friend at the "XXXXX" company's tech support line. He explained all this to me with great care and patience after I spent two minutes going through a telephone menu and 45 minutes "on hold," hearing how I was a very important customer to the company and would be helped within a few minutes.

Now there are obviously more questions you might have concerning this. One might be, "Will there be a difference in the amount of space needed on my hard drive if I scan an image at 300 dpi versus scanning it at 600 dpi?" Of course there will be a difference. The equation will have to take into account not only the dpi differences, it will have to factor in things such as whether you scan in black and white or color. I would imagine that all this would be a geometric progression, but I did not discuss this with Jonah, and suggest you check the manual that came with your scanner or call your tech support line.

Appendix C
Technical Assistance

The different image-editing programs mentioned in this book have a number of special download and technical support services that will help you if you need extra assistance.

With most of these programs you can even try a free "trial" version of the product. This means that you do not have to trust me when I say that these are good image-editing programs. You can try them out for yourself without spending any money!

Below is the information you need to contact these companies. Please note that you can always receive help "on-line" for free. However, most of these companies do not have toll free numbers. This means you will be paying something (either a flat fee or a long distance telephone charge) for their services.

Company	Web Site Address	Technical Support Number
ACDSystems	www.acdsystems.com	1-250-544-6701 (tech support)
Adobe	www.adobe.com	1-206-675-6358 (complimentary) 1-206-675-6126 (flat fee)
Jasc	www.jasc.com	1-800-622-2793 (customer care) 1-952-930-9171 (tech support) international numbers available
Microsoft	www.microsoft.com	1-425-637-9308

Needless to say, there are many other image-editing programs from other companies. By all means go to their Web sites and see if they have free trial versions that you might want to check out.

Glossary

This glossary includes more words and terms than you would normally expect in a book on basic digital image editing. In fact, there are some words that you will not find in the body of this book. I chose to include additional information as you might be reading articles or hearing terms that you do not understand. My thought is that this glossary can be a resource to you well past the first week with your new camera.

Acquire To place digital images onto the computer using hardware such as the camera with special cables, a memory card reader, a scanner, a CD, or by capturing images from the Internet.

Album A folder containing digital images. Note: It is best if you name and date these folders.

Aperture The opening in the lens of the camera that allows a measured amount of light to expose the film or memory chip. The size of the opening is described as a number and is referred to as the f-stop. The larger the f-stop number, the smaller the opening of the lens. If there is a lot of light, you will want a large or higher number, and if it is dark, you need a smaller or lower number so that the lens opening allows in the amount of light needed to capture the image correctly.

Archives The group of images that are saved in folders or files—a storage system. Often you will have so many albums that they take up a lot of space on your hard drive. These files can be compressed into archives and then viewed by decompressing the files. Other options include placing all the albums on a CD or adding a supplementary hard drive to your system. (As this is the first week, I would not worry about this too much.)

Artifacts The effects caused by the computer program trying to fill in missing pixels in an image that you are trying to enlarge. The program attempts to guess the missing colors in the best way that it can without the extra pixels. When you have fewer bits trying to represent more and more information, this produces a blotchy effect.

Aspect Ratio The ratio of the height to the width of an image.

Background The area behind the main image in a photograph.

Background Color When editing a digital image or creating special effects, you can create a special color for the background of the image. As an example, in Photoshop Elements there are two overlapping squares at the bottom of the toolbox. From a palette of colors you can choose whatever color you want to use for the background of your image—and for the foreground, too.

Batch Renaming A method of naming a whole group of images at one time. This is very useful if you need to organize some albums quickly and want a general name/category for the visit to Mannheim or Bad Kissingen before actually giving a separate name (David K.'s house) to each photograph.

Binary The numbering system that operates computer hardware and software. It refers to the fact that the only numbers used are "0" and "1."

Blurring The technique used to sharpen an image by softening the background. It works well for portraits, as it enhances the image of the person and decreases the influence of the area behind him.

BMP (Bit-Mapped File) Format The file format that was the original standard on Windows. BMP does not compress images at all. It is one pixel per pixel. Nothing is done to it. One of the main uses of this format today is for editing images and for the background or "wallpaper" on your computer desktop. It is not used on the Internet.

Brightness In digital editing, when you change this setting, *everything* in the image is either lighter or darker. The whole image is modified along the entire spectrum to either increase of decrease the light level. (Imagine that you are changing the image to see what it would look like at noon, and then at dusk.)

Browse To look for something—in this case an image—on your computer. The "Browse" tool helps you to find the folder in which you placed a photograph and then lets you view all the images in that folder as thumbnails. (See *Thumbnails.*)

Brush Tool In Photoshop Elements the tool that looks like a paintbrush and is used to digitally paint colors onto an image for special effects.

Brush Width One of the options you have when choosing the "Brush" tool. Not only can you choose from a number of widths, but you can also decide if you want the effect to be soft or hard.

Burn A technique used in photography to change the exposure of a particular area of an image. When burning an image, the exposure is increased to make an area darker. This is one of the tools available in some of the image-editing programs.

Byte The amount of space needed on a computer hard drive to represent a single character (eight bits). As this is a very small unit and many bytes are needed to handle most programs, terms for larger units have developed such as "kilobyte," "megabyte," and "gigabyte" (one billion bytes).

Captions Text that can be added to the image using an editing program.

CCD These initials stand for Charged Coupled Device. A CCD chip is a sensor and a computer chip that is a permanent part of your camera. The CCD registers the different levels of light entering the camera. The information from the CCD chip becomes electrical charges that go through the camera's microprocessor. The microprocessor then changes them into digital bits. These digital bits get stored on the memory card and are the pieces of data that make up a digital photograph.

CD-ROM An acronym for "compact disk read-only memory." A CD-ROM is a high-capacity storage device that can hold up to 650 megabytes of data. This is the equivalent of the information on 500 floppy disks or 300,000 pages of text. The information on the disk is permanent and cannot be changed.

CD-RW This is similar to a CD-ROM, but differs in that the "RW" stands for "rewritable." These discs can be used over and over again. The disadvantage of this method of archiving images is that you can lose all your information by overwriting the disc by mistake.

Clip Art Images available on CDs (for a small fee) or off the Web (for free) that can be used to enhance your work or project.

Clipboard A place on your computer where information is temporarily held after it has been copied or clipped from a document or other information source. This data can then be transferred to another location, such as another document or program.

Color This refers to the three primary colors used in digital imaging: red, green, and blue. The opposites of the colors are: cyan, magenta, and yellow. On a color wheel you can see where and how each of these colors overlap. Adjustments to the color in an image-editing program are made by moving a slide control to increase or decrease the amount of each color.

Color Inkjet Printer A type of printer that lays down ink through small jet nozzles. It is important to have a good-quality printer for photographic images and to use high-quality paper.

Command Button An element in a dialog box that carries out a specific action. Examples of command buttons are the "Cancel" button and the "OK" button.

CompactFlash Card A type of memory card for storing digital images; it's also called a CF card. There are several systems for information storage, and this is one of the more popular ones.

Compression A method used to take information and convert it into smaller digital files. A digital image in JPG format is a compressed file. Compressing files causes some loss of information.

Contrast This term is usually linked with "Brightness." As you increase the "Contrast" setting, the black areas of the image become "blacker" and the white areas become "whiter." Decreasing the contrast setting means that everything becomes more gray or dingier.

Crop To change the shape and size of an image. To crop an image is to take away the parts of the photograph that you do not want or need to see.

Database Any collection of related information or "objects" created, organized, and controlled by a database management system. (An example is the information gathered about each image as the photograph is originally taken, and as it is later edited.)

Delete To get rid of something. When you delete a folder on the computer it goes to the "Recycle Bin" and stays there until it is purged or restored. When you delete an image/photograph from your memory card, *it is gone forever!*

Depth of Field The area in an image that is in sharp or proper focus. This can vary depending on the aperture setting, the focal length used, and the distance from the camera to the subject.

Descriptions Additional information that is added to a file

Digital Zoom This is an electronic attempt to make an image *appear* to be larger. In fact, the only thing happening is that the pixels in the center of the viewfinder or LCD screen are processed so that the image seems to be larger. It is not the same as "optical" zoom, which really magnifies the actual image. (Note: This is important, as digital cameras are often sold with the emphasis on the combination of optical and digital zoom. It is the optical zoom that is really important.)

Disc An alternative spelling for "disk"; it usually refers to a CD.

Disk A magnetic surface that permanently stores information. The internal hard disk of most computers holds most of your information. Removable disks such as "floppy disks" or Zip® disks are used to back up, or save data from the hard disk.

Disk Drive The mechanism that reads and writes information from and to a disk. There are several types of disk drives, including floppy disk drives, hard disk drives, zip disk drives, and compact disk drives.

Dockable A term referring to moving and resizing toolbars or tool boxes to different areas within a window. It means that they are windows within the main window.

Dodge A technique used in photography to change the exposure of a part of an image. It is the opposite of "burn." When you dodge an image, the exposure is decreased to make an area lighter. This is one of the tools available in some of the image-editing programs.

Download To copy files from one computer or organizer to another using a network connection. Usually this refers to copying files from the Internet onto your hard drive. In this book it also means transferring your images from your camera to your computer and receiving images (photographs) that are sent to you over the Internet.

DPI Dots per inch—used in describing the capabilities of printers.

Drag or Dragging To move something, such as a folder, by holding down the left mouse button and sliding the mouse over until the object is in the desired position.

Drop-down List A list of commands from which to choose in a dialog box.

E-Mail A way of sending messages electronically from one person to another over the Internet or a network. Messages are sent almost instantly and can contain text, files, voice messages, graphics, and digital images. It is a means of communicating around the world at great speed.

Edge Filters A method used to improve the contrast around the edges of a portion of the digital image.

Editing Images The process of changing the qualities of a photograph to meet your visual needs and for artistic expression. (Note: always edit *copies* of your original image in case your artistic interpretations surpass your actual needs. If you want to start the process over again, it will help to have an original.)

"Esc" Key ("Escape" key) The key found on the top left side of the keyboard that is used to cancel an activity or process. When you want to stop an operation, this is the quick way to do it. It is *really* useful when you want to "undo" editing mistakes immediately.

Exposure The moment when light hits film or a CCD and creates a visual impression. (See *CCD*.)

Extensions Short "names" or abbreviations on the end of file names that help identify what program created the file. They are shown as a dot followed by a few letters.

FAQ The abbreviation for the words "frequently asked questions."

File A collection of information that is stored on a disk.

File Format A method of organizing information using a specific type of encoding. This allows you to place images in a particular type of file using one of a number of standard programs. The file format is indicated by an extension (a dot followed by several letters; see above) that tells the computer which program it needs to open in order for you to see the information. File formats provide universal standards so that images can be viewed on all computers.

File Name A description of some kind that identifies or describes a file. The key to this is that in order to access the file, the correct extension (the dot with several letters) must be added. Without the extension, there is no way of knowing what the information is and what program is needed to access the data.

File Size The amount of space or kilobytes used by an image or by a file. This is important, because it makes a difference as to the amount of memory needed to hold your photographic data on a memory card or the hard disk of your computer. The size of an image, and therefore the amount of memory needed to store it, depends on many factors, including the format, the resolution, the number of colors involved, etc.

Filters Devices that let you change your images. All of the editing tools described in this book are "filters" of some kind. There are hundreds of filters. In this book, filters are the types of devices that let you manipulate the image in a variety of artistic ways.

Flatbed Scanner A piece of hardware that transfers a document or image to a computer. It has a flat, horizontal glass plate on which to place the document or photograph. The difficulty in using this type of scanner for photographic images is that it cannot produce the best resolution when enlarging an original print.

Floppy Disk A data storage device that is made up of a flexible round plastic disk encased in a hard plastic case. Most PC floppy disks are 3.5 inches in size and store 1.44 megabytes or 2.88 megabytes of information.

Focal Length The ability of a camera lens to enlarge or magnify something. It is a measurement. It also is linked to the angle of views and depth of field. The more magnification, the larger the focal length, and the less angle of view. Or if you use a telephoto lens, there is a large focal length, but you see less of your image.

Folder A location on your disk where related files are stored.

Format (See *File Format* and *Extensions*)

Gamma Control The control that affects the middle tones of an image. By making corrections with the gamma control, you do not change the light and dark areas of the image. It only enhances the middle range of colors, or grayscale.

"Garbage In, Garbage Out" A popular saying that refers, in this case, to the fact that if you do not take care to produce the best image you can, you cannot expect miracles when it comes to editing the image.

GIFF (Graphics Interchange) Format This extension is pronounced "jiff." It is most often used on the Web as it allows for transparent backgrounds. It is a compressed file and can only project 256 colors.

Gigabyte 1,024 megabytes. The abbreviation for this is GB.

Grayscale A value, measured in terms of percentages, of the black tones (100 percent) and white tones (0 percent) as determined by the amount of black ink that is covering an area. There are 256 shades of gray, and each is given a value from black (at 0) to white (at 255). This is often used for special effects in image editing.

Hard Disk The main storage area for data inside the computer.

Hard Disk Drive The device that is actually used to store the data and programs in the computer. It consists of sets of magnetically coated disks, called platters, which are stored vertically and rotate up to 3,600 rpm. The unit is self-contained and sealed. (Note: The terms hard disk, hard disk drive, and hard drive are used interchangeably.)

HTM format A file extension used in Web page documents.

Hue Hue is most commonly understood as the name of a color, but it is actually the value of a color measured by the amount of transmitted or reflected light. It is measured on a color wheel.

Icon A small picture that represents something such as files, folders, images, programs, commands, and the like. Clicking on an icon is the way to access that item.

Images In this book, it is one of the words used as a synonym for photographs.

Image Editing The process of taking a photograph, or other digital image, and altering it in some way.

Image Resolution The actual sharpness of an image as seen on the monitor and when it is printed out. It is a type of measurement and a way of describing the quality of a printer, scanner, monitor, etc.

ISO (International Standards Organization) Number A way of standardizing the different speeds of film. Standard ISO numbers enable you to know the type of film you need to buy for different situations, and ensure that the film will be the same everywhere in the world. Numbers such as ISO100, ISO200, or ISO400 refer to the speed of the film, which relates directly to its sensitivity to light.

JPG (Joint Photographic Experts Group) Format A file format in which the data is compressed. For this reason it is a "lossy" format, meaning that some of the information is lost with each compression or change to the image. If you are printing a small image, the loss is really not noticeable. Image files in the JPG format have the advantage of taking up less space on memory cards and computer hard drives than files in other formats. This is the most popular form of image file for the recreational photographer. (The acronym is pronounced "jay peg.")

Jaggies A term that refers to the jagged, stair-step effect that is produced along the diagonal lines of a low-resolution image after it is enlarged. An image is made up of pixels. Each pixel occupies a certain amount of space. A high-resolution image uses a lot of pixels, and so enlarging the image does little to change its basic appearance. However, if very few pixels are available (a low-resolution image), then enlarging the image means that you can actually see each of the pixels along a diagonal line; they look almost like little square steps.

Keywords Some words or phrases that help you to identify and find your images once they are placed in albums or folders. (If you cannot find your image and do a search of some kind, it will help you if you have attached several descriptive words to each photograph.)

Layers A way of describing the actual method of editing images and creating projects in more advanced image-editing programs such as Photoshop Elements. An image can be reorganized so that it is composed of separate pieces of information, much like a multilayered cake. Each layer is edited individually and then stacked on top of the previous layer. In this way you can use a variety of individual images to form one single photograph.

LCD The part of the camera that looks like a television screen. It displays the image you are capturing and then lets you see the result immediately. This is one of the major advantages of digital photography. If you can see your image right away, you can decide if you want to keep it, or if you need to try this one more time. The acronym stands for "liquid crystal display."

Lightness A way of describing color as a value. White is considered a color with the most "lightness," while black has the least lightness.

Lossless File Format A format in which each picture pixel is mapped to one screen pixel. (See *GIFF* and *TIFT*.)

Luminance (See *Lightness*.)

Marquee The clearly defined area created when the cursor is dragged along an image. It is rectangular in shape and is bordered by a broken/dashed line. (Cropping an image produces a marquee so that you can see what part of the photograph you will keep.)

Megapixel One million pixels. In digital photography, the number of megapixels determines the resolution of your camera. The higher the number of megapixels, the more resolution you will have available for capturing fine details in photographs and transferring this data to large prints.

Megabyte 1024 kilobytes or more that a million bytes. The abbreviation is MB and is pronounced "meg."

Memory The place where data and programs are kept while they are in use.

Memory Cards The general term for a variety of media used to capture and save images with a camera and then to transfer these images to the computer.

Memory Card Readers A peripheral device that is attached to a computer and is used to transfer data quickly from a memory card to the computer.

Menu A list of commands that are available in the program with which you are working. By selecting options from the menus, you tell the computer or the camera what you want it to do.

My Pictures The folder in the "My Documents" folder of the C drive where you should store all your photographs. When you download images, the computer will ask you where you want to save these files. Make your life easy. Keep all of them in the one place that is easy to identify. (Even if you know that you want to work on these photographs immediately, save them to "My Pictures." You can always create a shortcut to this folder on your desktop.)

Noise Pixels that are randomly colored and grouped together in a particular area. This is often noticeable when you change the format of an image. Some editing programs use filters to eliminate this problem.

Opacity A measure of how "see through" an image will be, as determined by a special effect tool. If the opacity setting is 1 percent, then the image is transparent, and if it is 100 percent then you cannot see through it.

Optical Zoom A measure of the change of the focal length of the lens of a camera in order to magnify an image. The optical zoom truly magnifies an image, unlike the digital zoom. The higher the optical zoom number the camera has, the better.

Optics The lens or lenses that make it possible for light to pass through to a recording device that produces an image. The size, type, and quality of the lenses determine what kind of photograph you will be able to take and its quality.

Palette A tool that is used in Photoshop Elements. It is "grouped" in an area called the "palette well" and is basically an expanded editing, information, and help tool that is readily available. Palettes are opened and viewed as individual windows or as drop-down menus.

Pane A section within the active window on the desktop

"PHD" Camera A slang term for a camera that is very simple to use because everything can be set to function automatically. The letters do not stand for Doctor of Philosophy. They stand for "push here, dummy." The more recognized term for this type of camera is a "point and shoot" camera.

Pixel The smallest element of the picture that can have color and brightness. In simple terms it is like one tile in a mosaic or a marble sitting in the hole of a peg board.

Pixelation The result of enlarging an image to a size where all the pixels are visible.

Port A "socket" that allows you to connect hardware that is outside the computer to a circuit board within the computer. The circuit board then connects to the Central Processing Unit(CPU).

PPI Pixels per inch. It is interchangeable with DPI in its basic meaning in printing. It is used primarily in professional aspects of editing and conversions of files.

Program A set of instructions that tell the camera or computer what to do and how to do it. Programs are software and are also referred to as "peripherals."

Pull-down Menu These are hidden, vertical menus that are accessed from the menu bar. A pull-down menu allows you to access commands and features of that particular program. (See *Drop-Down Menu.*)

Red eye The effect created when a flash of light hits the retina in a human eye and the color of the retina is reflected back onto the image-capturing device. It is something that makes people look unnatural and unattractive in photographs, and therefore digital image-editing tools were created to fix it. (Animals often have retinas that are a different color than the human retina. So the red-eye effect can sometimes make a wonderful pet photograph—it turns our cats' eyes a brilliant turquoise.)

Resizing The process of changing the size of a digital image. The dialog box often will provide a number of standard choices for this, or you can pick any size you want.

Resolution The number of pixels per inch. A measurement that relates to the size of the image in relationship to the number of pixels captured in the image. The higher the resolution, the better the printed image, especially if you plan to make large prints. However, higher resolution also means that each image contains a lot of information and uses a great deal of memory.

Rotation Turning the image so that it is facing the way you would like to see it while working on it in a digital image-editing program. Often you might have the camera in the vertical position when taking a photograph. Viewing this image on a computer screen is difficult (it will appear sideways), so you might want to turn it to the right or left by 90 degrees. You can also do a "free" rotation, which is not limited to 90-degree changes. This is useful for making art projects.

Saturation The intensity or purity of image colors. It is measured on a scale of 0 to 100. For a vivid image you need to increase saturation. To make an image "grayer," you need to decrease saturation. (See *Vibrance.*)

Scanner A device that makes a copy of whatever is placed on its image-capturing glass plate. It copies an item by encoding information one line at a time and then sends the information to a computer as electrical data. There are special scanners that are made specifically for photographic images. The key questions to consider when buying a scanner are: at what resolution does it scan, and how much do I want to pay? (See *Flatbed Scanner.*)

Select To choose an item on a menu or to highlight something. The result is that some action will take place with the next command you give.

Sepia A method of making your images look "old-fashioned" by adding a bit of brown tint to the colorization.

Serial Port The connector or socket that is used to attach or "plug in" input and output peripherals such as a camera cable or memory card reader to the computer.

Shareware Software that is provided over the Internet for free for a trial period. If you continue to use the program, you are asked to pay a fee.

Shortcut Menu A list of keystrokes that give the computer commands just as if you clicked on an icon or selected a command from a drop-down menu. A very useful shortcut in digital editing is hitting the "Esc" (Escape) key to cancel an action.

Software The term used to describe programs, operating systems, applications, and the like. Basically, if it is visible and a piece of equipment, it is hardware. If it is invisible and coded information that runs the camera or computer, it is software.

Stitching A process that involves taking a group of images that are related to each other and blending them together to make a single photograph. This image looks like a very long panoramic view. Many digital editing programs have a stitching tool or feature.

Text Words. In this case, words that are added to a digital photograph or project to describe or enhance it. Most digital image-editing programs have a special tool that makes it easy to do this.

Thumbnails Small preview images of the actual photographs. When you are trying to find a particular photograph (that you did not label), it is easiest to "view" the images in a folder as thumbnails. If there are several thumbnails that might be the image you need, click on the thumbnail to see the full-size photo. (*Or*, alternatively, it is the hard bit of material that covers the top twenty-five percent of the end of your thumb and keeps growing even after you die.)

TIFF (Tagged Image File) Format A file format that can be read by both the Windows and Macintosh operating systems. It is noted for being a "lossless" format. This means that it gives you a photograph that contains 100 percent of the data that was available at the time the photograph was taken.

Timestamp date A specific piece of data that is attached to each image that you take and then edit. Originally it tells you when you took the photograph, and later it tells you the time and date of the latest edit.

Transitions The different techniques used to tie together images or scenes such as the blends used between sections of a movie or the fades and wipes used between images seen as slide shows.

214

Uploading The process of transferring images or information from your computer to the Internet. Once this is done, the information can be "downloaded" to other computers, either as e-mail attachments or as Web pages.

USB (Universal Serial Bus) The standard type of connection or interface between the different peripheral devices, such as the memory card reader, and the computer. USBs allow you to plug in hardware and use it right away without rebooting the computer.

Vibrance Another aspect of saturation. A " Vibrance" tool helps increase or decrease the intensity of color by making colors brighter or duller.

Web (See *World Wide Web*)

White Balance A correction or tool that is available on most cameras to compensate for the subtle differences in the image colors based on the available light sources. Each light source has a measurable "color temperature": daylight will have a warmer color temperature than a fluorescent lamp. Warmer colors have reddish-orange tones and cooler colors are bluish. Knowing this, you can set the camera to compensate for the differences. (See *"Garbage In, Garbage Out."*)

World Wide Web A portion of the Internet that connects graphical and multimedia information (words, pictures, video, and sound).

Zooming The process of changing the focal length of the camera lens so as to magnify the image. In digital editing it is also the process of enlarging the image so as to have a better view of different parts of the photograph. This makes it easier to see the corrections you are making.

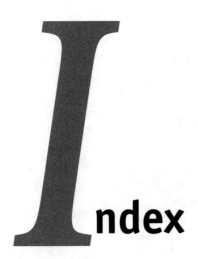

*I*ndex

Page numbers followed by an "f" indicate the presence of a figure.